THE ASPIRING SOLOPRENEUR

THE ASPIRING

SOLOPRENEUR

YOUR BUSINESS
START-UP
BIBLE

KRIS KLUVER

CHEROKEE STREET PUBLISHING

THE ASPIRING SOLOPRENEUR
Your Business Start-Up Bible

ISBN   978-1-5445-1259-4 *Hardcover*
          978-1-5445-1258-7 *Paperback*
          978-1-5445-1257-0 *Ebook*

To my loving wife, Reka, aka Little Miss Badass.

Your support and our life of adventure have made this possible.

CONTENTS

FOREWORD

———

This book will empower you to change your thinking from that of an employee to the mindset of an investor, manager, head of business development, and technician. This change in your thinking will allow you to confidently transition to becoming your own boss and living life on your terms. It's not just about getting by, but thriving.

I've been coaching and teaching leadership for nearly twenty-five years, and I've been blessed to have written a couple of *New York Times* best-selling books on the subject. My clients call me a leadership expert, but I blush when I hear those words. I like to refer to myself as a full-time student of leadership.

Last year, Kris attended one of my Heart-Led Leader retreats. I got to know his heart, and it's a good one. During this time together, I learned of Kris's dream to use his thirty-plus years as an entrepreneur to help others successfully transition from working for someone else as an employee to safely becoming a thriving solopreneur. His goal was to introduce a million people to a new way of thinking through this book, speaking events, online courses, and coaching.

I have to say...at first, this sounded ambitious. However, as I have gotten to know Kris, I've realized that the way he listens and approaches a challenge, combined with his real-life experience and genuine passion for helping people, is unique. Kris has started fourteen companies and has worked with hundreds of businesses. In reality, I think this book may have a much bigger impact than his current goal of reaching a million people.

Here's an example of Kris's thinking that directly impacted me. During the retreat, I shared with Kris my yo-yo weight problem. I told him all the diets I've been on. I told him about all the damn suit pants I own in my closet. We talked about this issue, and I asked his thoughts on diets, exercise, and health.

He didn't answer. He just listened.

A week later, Kris called me to talk about my questions around weight. He challenged me to consider if I was asking the right questions. Perhaps the questions shouldn't be *what* diet I should go on. Or *what* I should be eating. The question should be *why* do I overeat?

When he initially asked this, a long pause followed. I was trying to process his question. South Beach, Atkins, Jenny Craig, Weight Watchers, Paleo, and Ketogenic all told me *what* to eat. Kris asked me a completely different question...*Why* do I eat?

Remember, this is not a topic with which he has much experience, unlike entrepreneurship. But it's reflective of how he thinks differently and will push you to think differently too. As a friend, he had compassionately listened, challenged, and as a result, empowered me to think differently. Since that conversation, I've lost more weight than ever before and have kept it off. No more yo-yo. I've ditched the 34-, 35-, and 36-inch pants. I now proudly wear 32-inch pants.

Turns out Kris's *why* question changed my life and made me fall in love with this guy's heart. He cared enough to ask the hard questions.

And that's why Kris wrote *The Aspiring Solopreneur*—to ask the hard questions, empower change, and help others to think differently. There are hundreds of entrepreneurship books teaching the what and the how. But Kris starts off by asking about the why. Why do you want to be a solopreneur?

Kris's one question changed my life. This book is packed with a step-by-step process, encouragement, and questions that will change your life. Kris will take you on a journey where you will learn how to think differently, explore what's possible, and if it's right for you, confidently transition to your dream life as a solopreneur.

Enjoy the journey, and welcome to the revolution.

TOMMY SPAULDING, STUDENT OF LEADERSHIP, INTERNATIONAL SPEAKER, AND *NEW YORK TIMES* BEST-SELLING AUTHOR OF *THE HEART-LED LEADER* AND *IT'S NOT JUST WHO YOU KNOW*

WWW.TOMMYSPAULDING.COM

INTRODUCTION

—

Did you wake before your alarm and jump out of bed enthusiastic to go to work today? Or did you crush the snooze button and groan?

Having the freedom and flexibility to control and love your life while thriving in your work is within your grasp. Building this life is worth the time and energy it takes to get there.

If you currently feel professionally unfulfilled, want to find yourself, or struggle to get up and go to work each day, read on.

I've been in your shoes. I know your pain.

You've followed the career path as directed, taking one step and then the next. You've let the organization you work for dictate the terms of your employment and your professional success or failure. You are an expert in your field and great at what you do, but you've discovered that this organization's philosophies or approaches aren't really what you want. This internal conflict may arise around work-life balance, responsibility, growth potential, or one of a million other concerns or differences. Perhaps your parents wanted this path for you, or it happened to be an area you were naturally good at but you didn't really like. Maybe a friend told you, "That position pays well," and lacking another direction, you chose this path. Or you thought, "I don't know what I want to do, so this sounds good enough," and now you feel stuck. Maybe you want to try something completely new and different. Maybe you love your actual work, but you're in an environment you nearly despise. You hate sitting in the cube every day, and you feel undervalued. There's a glass ceiling you can never break through.

Welcome to office hell.

Everyone who lives it has their own version of office hell: it is the place you dread walking into every Monday through Friday, sometimes Saturday and even Sunday morning. You wake up and hit the snooze button because the last thing you want is to go into work.

Take a breath. Don't worry. There is a way out. The reality

is that we live in the most amazing and abundant time ever, and our success is only limited by our own thinking. We have never lived in a time when it was safer and easier to become a thriving, successful solopreneur.

I can hear some of you sighing and thinking, "Oh boy, this is going to be one of the New-Agey *you can do anything you set your mind to* books: all flash and no boom."

I do have a very positive attitude, and I do believe you can do anything. However, this book is *not* fluff. It will provide you with very specific steps, activities, and tools that you can use to be successful on your journey to becoming a solopreneur.

I know many people who look, from the outside, like they are living the dream. They make a ton of money, own just the right house and car, and take amazing vacations, yet they hate going to work. I have heard extremely dark stories of the dread people feel when stuck in office hell.

Long before you hit that point, consider a transition to an environment of freedom you can control. You may want to move to a new company or go back to school to get a new degree or trade—to do something, anything, different. You may daydream about being your own boss. You may be one of many professionals and technicians in every industry and trade who want to be in charge and not have to work for—or work with—others.

Like them, you want to run your own business as a *solopreneur*.

WHAT IS A SOLOPRENEUR?

A solopreneur is a business owner who works and runs their business solo—as in, mostly by themselves. They want to be accountable for themselves and their business without *having* employees or *being* an employee. It's one of the fastest-growing segments of the workforce because of the lifestyle and flexibility individuals can enjoy while solving a specific problem or filling a need. Times have changed, and a solopreneur life is not only possible, but it is embraced by millions. According to Quartz, it is estimated that 40 percent of America's workforce may be freelancers in one form or another by 2020*. The number has only continued to climb.

Examples include:

---

* Jeremy Neuner, "40% of America's Workforce Will Be Freelancers by 2020," Quartz, March 20, 2013, https://qz.com/65279/40-of-americas-workforce-will-be-freelancers-by-2020/.

Accountant	Architect
Attorney	Business Coach
Life Coach	Financial Planner
Counselor	Advertiser
Graphic Designer	Internet Technician
Therapist	Psychologist
Hairdresser	Massage Therapist
Aesthetician	Author
Contract Engineer	Tattoo Artist
Plumber	Jewelry Designer
Real Estate Agent	Loan Officer
Consultant	Chef
Pilot	Interior Decorator
Yoga Instructor	Fitness Trainer
Pilates Instructor	Chiropractor

...and many more. These are just to name a few.

Solopreneurs work on their own terms. Because of the current tax structures and challenges with providing healthcare, it may be cheaper for a corporation to contract with an outside "hired gun" at a higher rate than an employee. This strategy can often save an organization money in total employee costs, even though they pay a contracted solopreneur at a higher rate than they would pay an internal employee on salary. The company doesn't have to pay into your retirement, workman's compensation, insurance, or vacation time. As an independent solopreneur contractor, you can typically earn a higher wage and use the financial advantages to write off your own healthcare with tax-free dollars. (*Note: I am not giving you legal or tax advice. Please consult with an accountant and attorney for specific benefits and details. Really, I am not kidding here, my attorney friends would have an aneurysm if they thought I was giving "legal" advice. I prefer to think of it as "life" advice based on all the lessons learned from the things I have done wrong and much that went right.*)

Recent years have seen a massive increase in the number of people joining the solopreneur movement. Technological advances provide solo experts the tools to research and build successful businesses. You now have the ability to professionally communicate, transfer information, and market yourself to others seamlessly across the country. You can be an absolute guru in a very small niche and still get in front of the tribe of people that value your skills, anywhere in the world.

LIVE LIFE ON YOUR TERMS

Solopreneurs are driven by the desire to live life on *their* terms and safely transition into a life they love. Those terms are different for everyone, but it's important to define them up front so that you can determine if the solopreneur life is for you. To begin, you will explore and define your idea of personal success, identify your motivations, and assess the competitive environment in the first chapters of this book. Knowing this is key because you will be in charge. Once you know what success looks like for you, you can set your course and take the first steps toward your goal.

Motivations can be different for everyone. Some people want the ability to see every one of their child's soccer games or speech tournaments. Others want to work the usual forty to fifty hours a week but determine when those hours are. For example, someone who loves golf or riding her bike might want to work late at night. If so, he can work for a few hours in the morning, play golf or go on a bike ride, be home by 5:00 with the family, and then work again from 8:00 to 11:00 p.m.

Some people want to make more money but feel restricted in their current work environment. Although they work more hours than anyone else, they aren't bringing more money home. They know how much the company bills their time out to clients, and they can do the math, but they are salaried and feel stuck. They know the senior guys and owners are getting big bonuses that are based on their work.

Others want to work less or are stepping back into the game after being gone for an extended period of time. I see this a lot when people are looking for work-life balance or their youngest child has started kindergarten or left for college. It may be easier to create a job as a solopreneur, where they can work fifteen to thirty hours a week and earn $30-300 or more an hour, than to find a job with the same parameters.

As a solopreneur, you choose the lifestyle and direction, define your goals and plans, and drive your success. My wife and I love adventure travel, and I can honestly say every time I pull out my device and do a little "work" from a hut in the Italian Alps or a fishing camp in Alaska, I feel like I am getting away with something. Remember, as a solopreneur, you're the boss.

Whatever your motivation, defining it is the first step that will dictate your path. It's important to understand the pros and cons of being a solopreneur. As soon as you stop being an employee, you have to be accountable for all that you're doing. You may discover that all that "money" that you thought the boss held back from you was really going to overhead and expenses, and they weren't as profitable as you may have originally thought.

Get ready to change your thinking and embrace the idea that as a solopreneur you are accountable for everything that is involved in your business.

To be successful, you need to think like an investor:

investing in your business. You need to think like a manager: managing the business. You need to think like the head of business development: driving the business. And you need to be the technician working in the business, providing the actual service.

WHY DOESN'T EVERYONE BECOME A SOLOPRENEUR?

Being a solopreneur is not for everybody, but it can be great. The following chapters will show you what it takes to be successful, the potential financial start-up exposure, time requirements, and technical skills needed, and help you determine whether you should make the shift to being a solopreneur. I will go through each step in detail; however, before you turn in your resignation, I would encourage you to have an open, potentially hard and honest conversation with yourself to determine if going solo is the right direction for you. If you can answer "Yes" to the following two questions, solopreneurship may be for you.

ARE YOU WILLING TO LEARN NEW SKILLS?

The reality is that some people just aren't cut out to be a business owner.

They may be highly educated. They may be great technicians. However, they're one-trick ponies, great at only one thing, and typically, the skills it takes to be a great technician are rarely the same skills needed to launch and grow a business. Herein lies one of the primary reasons people get into trouble when they shift to being a solopreneur. You can be an amazing strategist, therapist, financial planner, accountant, attorney, or dentist, but the skillset it takes to be an expert has virtually nothing to do with the skillset to be a business owner. To run a successful business, you will need to act and think like an investor, manager, and head of business development, while remaining a great technician.

Can you learn these skills? Absolutely. But the challenge becomes deciding whether developing those skills is the right investment of your time. Just because you *can* doesn't always mean you *should*.

In some cases, you may be able to outsource the areas that aren't your strengths. That is fine, but you will need to factor this into the amount of money you need to charge clients to cover those expenses. When you factor in the additional costs, you will need to assess the viability of your idea, define what you will be able to charge, and determine what you need to charge. These are just a few of the decisions a solopreneur has to make. You'll evaluate them later in this book.

ARE YOU *REALLY* A SELF-STARTER?

Some people may not like where they currently work or dislike the idea of having a boss, but in reality, they wouldn't get anything done if the boss didn't tell them what to do. You must answer honestly when you ask yourself, "Am I a self-starter?"

This can be another major factor in the failure of so many solopreneurs. When going out on your own, you may commit your life savings, stress marital relationships, and engage in the most challenging journey of your life. If you stink at follow-through or self-motivation, *be honest* with yourself. Some people aren't capable of pushing themselves, and they know they ultimately won't follow through to get the task or project done. *That's okay.* Embrace this discovery. Own it. Be the best technician you can, and if you hate the environment where you currently work, find a place that you will love. If you love what you do but hate your boss, no one is holding a gun to your head to stay. Start looking for a place, and a boss, that you will love.

NERVOUS ABOUT BEING A SOLOPRENEUR?

Good. It's okay to be nervous and cautious. As human beings we typically fear the unknown and change. Starting a new business is scary, and the reality is that the majority of start-ups fail. They go down in flames, some taking life savings and trusted relationships with them. A high percentage—somewhere between 30 to 50 percent—of companies fail within the first five years. What most people don't talk about—and what I firmly believe—is that 50 percent or more of the remaining businesses flatline, stagnate, and, at best, bump along solely based on the owner's determination and stubbornness. Surviving is not thriving. This is no way to move forward; life is too short to just survive. You deserve to thrive, and I will show you how.

Why do these terrible statistics happen? There are many reasons, but I believe a lack of education, research, preparation, and candid personal acknowledgment around the start-up process are the major factors. Almost never is it because someone is not a great technician. Some people don't know where they're going or how they're going to get there. Many people simply spin their wheels in frustration. Whose fault is that? I will tell you: it is that person in the mirror. Others keep throwing money at shortcomings and problems in hopes of changing, even when they shouldn't. Hope is a crappy strategy. Eventually they turn a corner or run out of money. None of these are good options. There is no need for this, and I will walk you through the steps to avoid these traps.

There are so many success stories too. Some businesses do thrive. People do what they love and help people in ways that they love. They live their ideal life, achieve their financial dreams, and fulfill their personal motivations.

LEARN HOW TO SAFELY TRANSITION AND THRIVE

Now—take a deep breath and relax. *You don't have to be one of the awful statistics.* This isn't untrodden territory. The reality is, successful businesses have been started millions of times over, and many of these owners are available to help you capitalize on your expertise and build your business. There is a huge number of business owners who really, truly, want to help you be successful. There are experts in accounting, law, insurance, and banking whose main goal is helping you be successful. (In the second part of this book, I will cover how to build your team of advisors by finding them, interviewing them, and best leveraging their skills.)

One of the biggest challenges solopreneurs faced in the past was operating alone, in a bubble, and not knowing what they didn't know. Today, the solopreneur community is not only growing to directly help businesses and individuals, but there is an army of expert entrepreneurs and solopreneurs that exist to help other solopreneurs. This community of experts helps others like them to be successful. The tide has shifted and, even as a solopreneur, you don't have to do it all alone.

This is one of the primary reasons I wrote this book. The website aspiringsolopreneur.com was created to educate and empower others to become thriving solopreneurs. Users can find tools, resources, and an online community to celebrate the solopreneur lifestyle and support each other's growth, including the Solopreneur Success Certification Courses, Online Solopreneur Success Camps, and private coaching and advisory services.

When done right, owning and operating a business and living the path to achieving your dream is an amazing experience. Once you find your groove, it can be easy to do. In fact, it's never been easier. There are now more tools at your fingertips, immense resources for researching and vetting ideas, dozens of ways to test your concept, and clear options to safely transition into a new life— before you ever leave your existing position. I believe we are in a golden age; solopreneurship is the easiest and safest it has been in the history of mankind.

Together we will:

1. Identify your motivations and what success looks like for you.
2. Determine what aspects of your current work you love and why.
3. Assess how this need is being solved and identify your unique niche.

4. Interview others and assess the market conditions.
5. Outline a success road map.
6. Learn how to find, interview, and build a team of expert advisors:
   A. Accountant
   B. Attorney
   C. Insurance expert
   D. Banker
7. Build a success guide that contains your list of advisors, completed road map, financial viability, initial timeline to launch, and defined accountability.
8. Review and assess the plan and make adjustments if needed.
9. Execute the timeline for a smooth and successful transition and launch.
10. Create the discipline to become a solopreneur.
11. Navigate the first six months like a pro.

None of these steps are particularly difficult, but you will need to do the work. When each step is completed fully and with honesty, you will dramatically increase your likelihood for success.

WHY TRUST ME?

Entrepreneurship is what I do. It's how I am wired. Today, I spend the majority of my time working with entrepreneurs, helping them achieve their dreams through different strategic processes, candid feedback, and education. I've had successes and failures, and it's honestly through the latter that I learned the most. My knowledge is not theoretical, my knowledge is actual in-the-trenches, getting-clobbered, and figuring-things-out knowledge. This gave me a front row seat to the transformational power of the employee-to-solopreneur move. I have the experience and the battle scars. Not only do I have this expertise, but I enlist the help of others as well. Throughout this book I will share expert interviews from the people I trust and surround myself with.

I started my first of fourteen companies when I was nineteen years old, but I actually began mowing lawns and shoveling snow when I was twelve. One way or another, I've been self-employed for close to forty years. Over that time, I have built, bought, sold, occasionally run into the ground, and owned a wide variety of companies in marketing, real estate development, retail, consulting, professional services, coaching, mortgage services, and others. When I was a business broker, I crawled inside hundreds of different businesses and got to see the good, the bad, and sometimes the ugly. I bought them, sold them, advised them, and started them from scratch.

When I started in the late 1980s, *entrepreneurship* was a dirty word. If you said you were an entrepreneur, this basically guaranteed you were never going to get a job in the corporate world. Once you started on this path, you were on your own. I was in one of the first university entrepreneurship programs in the country. I have been alone in that start-up desert, and I believe it is my calling to ease that path for others. My goal now is to help change people's lives. I want to save people's lives, marriages, and money, and empower them to live their dream and find success on their terms. I want to empower and help people to thrive, not survive. I am a senior advisor to CEOs ranging from billion-dollar organizations to small start-ups. I've worked with hundreds of different organizations and individuals. My experiences have given me a front row seat to the transformational power of the employee-to-solopreneur move. I've seen firsthand how rewarding and life-changing the journey can be when an individual professional makes the successful transition to owning and operating their first business.

Today you have the ability to live any life you want. Your thinking is the only inhibitor of your dreams and of achieving those dreams. You can be and do anything. Reka, my wife, and I are examples of what the solopreneur life can look like. We are living the life of our dreams. We take a total of three months off a year, spread out about a week each month for adventures, and one full month to live somewhere overseas. We are humbled to work with people we want to work with. We're privileged to be helping people we want to help. We are grateful because we have discovered our purpose. We plan to keep working until the day we die because we love what we do, and we love having an impact on others. I get to go to work. To embrace these beliefs, and remind myself of them every day, I have tattoos with the infinity symbol and the words *abundance* and *gratitude*. I know that is a little on the hippie-voodoo side of things, but it works for me and is a constant reminder that living the life of your dreams is worth the work it takes to get there.

ESTABLISH TRUE NORTH

Just as the hand on the compass always points north, I live by and run my business by a core group of principles I call my True North—which I share further in chapter one.

I draw on those principles specifically to help you, the reader, find your happiness, adventure, and self-confidence. Through this journey, there's a chance I will help you decide that being a solopreneur is *not* the best option for you. I still consider that a victory because this knowledge will help you to potentially save your life savings, your marriage, your health, or all of the above. Your journey through this process may help you decide that your job isn't so awful, or that all you need is a change of employment. My intention is that if you move forward into the journey of solopreneurship, you do so with eyes wide open; your path is clear, and your likelihood for new-found success on your terms is very real.

My goal is not to convince you to do anything. I love what I do, but that is my life. If you choose a different path to a solopreneur life, I couldn't respect you more. This is not for everyone. I don't want everyone to convert to solo-preneurship; rather, I want to create an awareness of this opportunity, introduce a road map, and empower people to thrive. For some, the journey alone will light up your brain. It will get you thinking and looking at things in a completely different way. We will help adjust and expand these thoughts, and you will see opportunities abound. What kind of opportunities? Business, niche, and areas to thrive in your best life.

When you start this solopreneur journey, you may think that one path is where you're headed, but the fact that you're opening up your mind to this opportunity could result in another path. You never know what will happen, but adjusting your thinking allows you to become aware of available opportunities. You will potentially see differ-ent paths, different industries, and different niches. Part of our process together is that change in thinking: to be more of an investor, manager, head of business devel-opment, and technician. The investor will make sure the business is viable and the financial investments align with the goals and *need to haves* for the company's success. The manager will make sure that the technician stays on task and delivers the product or service on time and within budget. The head of business development is the one who ensures you actually have work to do and helps build the relationships. And, of course, the technician is the one doing the job!

This process will also help you to start becoming aware of all the opportunities that exist. We live in such an abundant time! Within these pages you will find my step-by-step process to researching, launching, and growing a solo start-up. You will identify what success looks like on your terms. You'll receive advice and direction on much of what a small business owner needs to know. You'll learn from my own experiences as well as expert interviews. More importantly, you will begin to fully understand the tools needed to slowly and safely transition from being a great technician in someone else's organization to owning and operating a great business that you own, manage, and work in as a great technician. These are the same tools used in the Solopreneur Success Certifications and Solopreneur Success Camps. Members get one-on-one coaching or virtual-based group coaching, accountability, and a road map to follow. You'll get the same information here for just the price of the book.

Let's get started.

PART ONE

IDENTIFY MOTIVATIONS AND ASSESS THE MARKET

CHAPTER ONE

IDENTIFY YOUR WHY

Success is not the key to happiness. Happiness is the key to success. If you love what you are doing, you will be successful.

ALBERT SCHWEITZER

People look at success differently today than they did a hundred years ago. And a hundred years from now, it will be viewed differently again. Everyone defines success on their own terms. For you, success may be defined as more time with your family or flexible work hours. You get the opportunity to define success on your terms and do whatever you choose. If you want to work twenty-three hours a week, and most of them in the middle of the night, you can do that! As a solopreneur, you are the driver, and your success comes on your terms. Part of the beauty of being a solopreneur is that you no longer have to fit inside someone else's box. You're taking the opportunity to step outside—a step few people take—and it can be scary and intimidating.

You have the control and ability to do whatever you want, and I want to help you identify the cornerstones of what success looks like specifically for you. In order to define your success, you have to take a step back and look at what matters most to you, assess whether your life is in balance, define your True North, and define your *why*.

ASSESS LIFE BALANCE

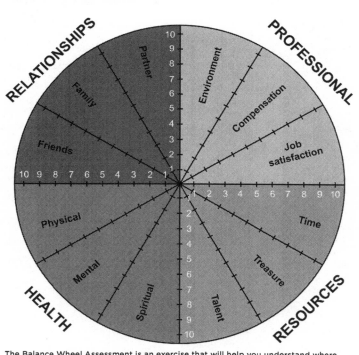

The Balance Wheel Assessment is an exercise that will help you understand where key aspects of your life are solid, and where others may be out of balance.

As Albert Schweitzer says, "Happiness is the key to success." Whether you're a solopreneur or not, a balanced life is critical for your happiness. If you have a great partner, great family, and great friends, but you have no money and you're not healthy, you're probably not as happy as you think. If you have a great job but no free time, and your partner just left you, you're probably not happy, either. If you have all the money in the world, but nobody wants to talk to you because you're always at work, for most, that's not happiness either.

The Balance Wheel Assessment helps you determine what a balanced, happier life looks like to you and where you may currently have strengths or opportunities. By answering questions about four areas of your life—your relationships, your professional life, your resources, and your health—you can see where you are currently strong and perhaps where you can focus your energies to improve.

If you have an imbalanced score, what changes could you make in your life that would create balance? Think about how being a solopreneur will help you raise the score in the area you would like to focus on.

Most of you already know what you are looking for; however, this tool is intended to aid you to think outside the box, to identify what success looks like—on your terms—and help you become aware of other possibilities. There's a full Balance Wheel Assessment and review in the appendix or online at aspiringsolopreneur.com.

I believe it is important to start with the assessment and keep the results top of mind as you build your new life. If you feel you are crystal clear about where you're going, you can skip it, but if you want to explore the assessment, be open and honest with yourself when you work through it. You will begin to see trends, opportunities, strengths, and what life outside of "office hell" could look like. You'll also be able to recognize the areas you value, where you are doing well, and any areas of opportunity where you could improve.

DEFINE TRUE NORTH

For the aspiring solopreneur, you can't begin your journey until you are clear on who you are—your own True North. Jim Collins, author of *Good to Great,* calls it your *core values.* Other names may include core beliefs, personal morals, character, individual ethics, passions, or personal values. When you first invest the time to determine your True North, and then your *why*, you can then build on these fundamentals to identify and crystallize what is really important to you and your best path forward to success and happiness.

The True North acts as your guiding direction and provides a set of principles that can help you decide if you should embark on this solopreneur journey. As an example, here are mine:

- **Embracing life as an adventure:** I've had the good fortune to have visited all seven continents and nearly fifty countries. I met my wife while traveling on a freighter in Chile. I look at everything as a journey, even this entire process. I look at every mundane day as an adventure. I embrace the good and bad in everything that's there. It's a constant position of positivity and excitement.
- **Fearlessly giving first for the betterment of others:** I always want to do the right thing, even if it's not what people want to hear. I want to be the person who will empower and help people.
- **Always curious/learning:** I am a huge fact finder. I love learning and believe that I can learn something special from everybody, from a small child tying their shoes to the way the garbage man enjoys his job.
- **Living a philosophy of gratitude and abundance:** I believe in the idea of abundance, the philosophy of giving, and gratitude. We are one of the first generations that doesn't have to spend most of our time worrying about surviving; we can thrive. We live in an amazing time.
- **Owning your life experience, attitude matters:** I own my actions, my words, and my intentions, and

what I say is what I mean. I am truly accountable for the good and the bad, and my attitude impacts others and myself.

Realize that what I've outlined is based on my experiences and my values and is intended to provide you with an example. It may not have anything to do with your dream or the direction you want to take. Just as everyone should define success in their own way, each of us has a personal True North; I want you to find yours. Your outcome will be unique to you. It will be a reflection of what's most important to you and allow you to build a solopreneur model to fit your beliefs and *not the other way around*. More often than not, people build the business first and then try to fit their True North around it. This approach typically ends in friction rather than synergy.

The act of clarifying your True North and embracing the statements as your fundamental beliefs will help guide your direction. Document your first draft here:

....

....

....

....

....

....

....

....

....

....

....

You may have gone through a similar exercise in another book or course and already know what your True North is. However, if you haven't or you would like to review and reaffirm what you believe your True North to be, you can do so at aspiringsolopreneur.com. There, you will go through the same exercise people go through in my personal and couple goal-setting retreats.

Note: This exercise is only one of two that I don't provide in the book. While I believe they are important to your overall direction, I don't want them to be a distraction. Likely you bought this book because you already have a good idea of what you want to do. Don't worry, everything else you need for launching your solopreneurship is here! I know I personally hate it when I buy a book and find it to be a giant commercial for someone's website. This is not the case. I promise.

DEFINING YOUR WHY

You've looked at your life balance and reinforced your True North. Your Balance Wheel shows you how you prioritize your personal relationships, your profession, your resources, and your health. Your True North reflects your values and who you are at your core, but the next step, the *why*, will help define what floats your boat, what lights you up and makes you happy. This step is equally important to the previous two and assesses *why* you're looking to embark on the solopreneur journey.

If you already know your *why*, jump ahead to the home-work at the end of this chapter and document it. If you're unsure or want to explore further, this activity will help.

To begin determining your *why*, start looking at the aspects of what you love and hate about your current job. Get specific and drill down. If you love going to work, list the things you love about it. If you really hate going to work, list all the things that make you feel that way.

LOVE	HATE

It's within that love and hate that you begin to identify your motivations. If you love talking with people, that's wonderful and important to know. This may suggest that you like the personal interactions of your work. If you hate attending meetings and dealing with your company's bureaucracy, this might suggest that you would really prefer to be your own boss or that you just hate having to do the day-to-day paperwork. As you go through each item ask yourself, "Is this what I really love or hate, or is this more of a symptom of what I really love or hate?" You may think you love it when people come to you with questions, but what you actually love is being a problem-solver or being a teacher. Continue to narrow down the scope and identify these motivations so you can start to see ways to focus and amplify them in the solopreneur world. You have options. Nobody is making you stay in your current situation. If you want a different life, this is where you begin the journey. The biggest inhibitor of dream achievement is your own thinking, and it all begins with getting clear on your motivations. It's time to determine what floats your boat and begin to think positive and dream big! Take the time to think about *why* you like doing one thing or another, not just the specific *what* it is you are doing.

TIME, TREASURE, AND TALENT

The second key ingredient in motivation is your outside factors. Previously, I talked about your internal motivations, and now I will review the external motivators that can affect you.

When readers first begin to identify their motivations and why they want to escape office hell, they usually come up with answers like freedom, money, time, flexibility, proving someone wrong, pride of ownership, and so on.

Those are all valid, but I find that, ultimately, these external motivations boil down to what I like to call the three main Ts: time, treasure, and talent. These are the only three things in the world you can leverage. If you're having trouble defining your motivation, look at time, treasure, and talent and identify what you want to build upon or where are you lacking. It could be one, two, or all three of them.

- **Time:** Time is minutes and hours spent doing what you love. If you want to be able to go to every one of your daughter's recitals, one of the motivations for being a solopreneur is being able to control your time on your terms. Whether it's a controlled office environment, hating a daily commute, or ineffective meetings, there is a long list of commitments that can rob you of precious hours. This loss of control can have major impacts on your relationships, health, and your overall well-being.

- **Treasure:** Treasure is money and stuff! Many people feel undervalued or poorly rewarded or believe they could or should be doing work with a higher value. Value and recognition for your work comes in many forms, but compensation is a very real indicator. Over time, feeling you are not getting paid what you are worth becomes demotivating. Knowing your worth and getting compensated accordingly is a wonderful feeling.

- **Talent:** Talent is your God-given abilities and any skills you've been able to embrace. You may want to use your talent to help others in a way your current position doesn't allow. Or you may want to grow your talents and fulfill an inner desire to maximize your personal development in a completely different field.

The internal and external motivations will be completely unique to you, and each motivation may have its own reason. I want to have more time for adventures. I want more treasure, but I need to accomplish that by lever-

COMPLETE CAREER CHANGE

In some cases, an aspiring solopreneur may be looking to make a dramatic career change. This can be both exciting and terrifying all in one shot. And it is 100 percent possible.

My wife, Reka, is the daughter of Mauritian immigrants who live in London. (Mauritius is a tiny country in the Indian Ocean. I had to look it up!) Reka is excellent with numbers and a gifted student; she was the first in her family to attend college and obtained a degree as an accountant. Even though she was an excellent accountant with a job in London with a venture capital firm, she hated accounting. She showed up each day for work because it was what she thought she was supposed to do. It was her responsibility. Her family was proud of her because she was "successful" and had a "good" job. But Reka was not happy; she was living her version of "office hell."

At age forty, she embarked on a seven-year journey to find a new path. It involved a lot of work, research, and time. She ultimately decided to return to school to become a couples and family counselor because counseling had made a positive impact on our relationship and helped her deal with her childhood. She wanted to give back and help others, and she had the desire, the empathy, and the skillset to be a counselor. She shifted her direction, returned to school, and earned her master's degree. Today Reka is a successful solopreneur who owns her own practice and, as a result, she makes better money than she did as an accountant, works about twenty hours a week in a field that she loves with people she likes, and still takes three months of vacation a year. She identified her *why* and her True North, and the work she does now is very much in alignment with that. She's very happy with the results.

You can do the same.

aging my time better. I live a simple life and have an appreciation for nice things. Because of my True North and my personal wiring, I always want to be learning and increasing my talents.

Document your top three motivations for *why* you want to become a solopreneur:

....

....

....

HEALTHY MOTIVATORS

Now that you've determined your *why*, ask yourself if your motivators are healthy. You wouldn't believe the number of people who do things for the wrong reasons.

Perhaps you currently have a boss or co-worker who berates you and tells you—and everyone who will listen—that you could never be your own boss. A possible motivation may be to prove her wrong. While this could be a *valid* motivation, I would ask you to consider if it's the *right* motivation. Are you willing to throw your life into turmoil just to prove some idiot wrong?

If you do something for the wrong motivations, your successes will be hollow. This doesn't mean you shouldn't explore the notion of going out on your own, but it's better if the motivations are forward moving and tied to personal growth rather than externally fueled. If you desire more control and accountability of your work life, with the ability to have flextime and make all your daughter's dance recitals, that is a positive motivation. When you succeed, you can still let the former office bully know what an idiot they were.

The key is knowing your motivation and then owning it. Make sure you're aware of it because that will be one of the points that will help you define success. Bring your motivation full circle, and you'll be looking at it from the side of success.

PARTNER ALIGNMENT

Once you've identified your True North and your *why* motivation, share this with your partner/spouse. It's critical that your partner understands where you are coming from, what is important to you, and why you are looking to become a solopreneur. You need to be on the same page.

Your choices will have a major impact on those closest to you. This can be a very scary time for your partner, so it is critical to empower them to understand your goals and reasoning.

As an example, when I was a business broker, if the buyer intended to get a small business loan, I would require that I meet with the buyer and the partner/spouse. Most small business loans require a personal guarantee and some form of collateral, most often in the form of the buyer's home. Early on in my career, I had more than one deal go sideways when a partner/spouse found out last minute and went bananas: "You are putting the house I raised my kids in on the line for this business idea of yours?"

Having the discussion early is important. If you need to go back to school, can you afford the expense and lack of income? Does your partner/spouse need to return to work or change jobs for a higher salary? Do you need to downsize for a while? I will go over all the requirements needed to transition into solopreneurship, but keeping your partner/spouse involved is key.

If you announce, "I know I am currently an accountant, but I'm not happy, so I'm going to become an expert in couples and family counseling, quit my job, and start my own practice," expect some pushback! A better way to bring it up would be, "Look, I've been working through what is important to me and what I want to do with my career. I would like to explore becoming a couples and family therapist. I don't know if it is right for me, but I do want to learn what it would take and what the path entails to get there. I believe I would be great at it, and it would make me happy. I know I will need to do a ton of research and likely have to go back to school, but I really want to explore this, and I need your support to help me determine if this is a good fit for me and for us. And, by the way, nothing will be changing today, except that I will start to do my research."

Boom! Now you have your first advocate and person on your support team. Clearly understand where you're going, confidently express your expectations, and share your research and plan to ensure the success of your venture. This will vastly minimize your partner's concerns and make it easier for him or her to be supportive and flexible. Well done.

THE RIGHT THINKING

Remember that nobody's making you stay in your situation. Current social attitudes encourage a victim-based mentality, and a successful solopreneur or entrepreneur is never victim-based. You are always accountable to yourself. Nobody requires you to go to work. There certainly may be repercussions if you stop going to the office, but you must embrace personal accountability. If you want to change your current situation, you can.

The biggest inhibitor of dream achievement is your own thinking. Do you look at things with a philosophy of "I can't" or "I can"? In the words of Yoda, "Do. Or do not. There is no try." If you decide you're going to do something, then *you can do it*. Making a change may not always make sense and may not always be the best option, but you can do almost anything you can dream.

A successful change starts with being crystal clear on the outcome you want to achieve. From there, you will break it down into the vital steps to meet that goal. These smaller components allow you to clearly see the path for making the change, and that's what we'll be doing to transition your career to a successful solopreneur life.

This part of the process is incredibly empowering but can be time consuming. It takes time and a lot of internal reflection to determine your True North and motivation for considering a shift to becoming a solopreneur. Taking the time now will benefit you substantially as you go further down this process. I want to make sure that you are on a path to create an environment in which you will thrive—both in work and your work-life balance. You will know your exact goal as you create the path to achieve it. You will be in control of your own life.

That's it for the hippie voodoo stuff! Are you ready to dive in and start changing your life now?

TAKEAWAYS

- Life balance is the key to happiness, and happiness is the key to success.
- Knowing your True North will help guide your direction.
- Embracing your genuine motivations will help you discover your *why*.
- Your motivations are often rooted in the three Ts: Time, Treasure, and Talent.

HOMEWORK

As we go through the book, there will be homework at the end of each chapter. I would urge you to be diligent about completing each step and trust there is a method to the madness. I suggest you keep it all in one place—either electronically or in an old-school three-ring binder. You can also go to aspiringsolopreneur.com and order a workbook with premade tabs and pages.

1. Define where and how you will store your work and begin with these exercises.

2. Draw your Balance Wheel.

3. Document your True North.

....

....

....

....

....

4. Document your *why.*

....

....

....

....

....

CHAPTER TWO

IDENTIFY YOUR WHAT AND WHO

—

You do not merely want to be considered just the best of the best. You want to be considered the only one who does what you do.

JERRY GARCIA

Chapter one helped you determine your True North and define your *why* for becoming a solopreneur. In this next step, you will begin to narrow down your *what* so you know what you want to do to fulfill your *why*.

Once you know your *why* and *what*, you can pursue your dream in a way that you become not only exceptional at what you do, but your clients will happily compensate you for your time and expertise.

How do you start to define your *what*? This involves three key questions:

1. What is the specific problem you are helping to solve? You will learn this by identifying your target client and drilling down on what, specifically, they need help with.
2. How is this need currently being solved? You learn this by assessing the marketplace and how others are going about their solutions.
3. What is unique about your ability to solve it? You learn this by identifying your unique value proposition and outlining how you will address it.

Your thinking here may have a cyclical evolution. You may go through the process in this chapter multiple times to further define and narrow your scope.

IDENTIFY YOUR TARGET CLIENTS

Most people solve a problem by examining their competitors and trying to copy what they do. I suggest that you start by talking with the real people who will use your product or service. If you currently have clients and you're comfortable talking to them, great. If not, let's define what your ideal client looks like.

Imagine someone calling your cell phone. You see the name and you think, "It's Smiling Sally. I love talking to Sally! She is easy to work with, pays on time, values my work, and we have fun together." You pick up the phone immediately.

Now stop—why do you love talking to Sally? What attributes does she possess? What are you doing for her? What does she value? Get specific; these are the initial descriptors for your ideal client.

If Sally recommended you to someone else, why would she do that? "I love working with <your name here> because ___." The words that follow "because" hold the real gold of the differentiation you offer.

Now on the flip side, imagine the phone rings and it's "Grumpy Gus." You think, "Oh no. He drives me crazy. His check clears, but it is usually late. He always complains and tries to chisel more out of me." You sigh and pick up the phone. Remember, you are not looking to survive; you want to thrive! Assess this person's attributes and why you dislike working with Grumpy Gus—knowing who you don't want as a client is as important as knowing your ideal client.

These are defining moments, and you'll use these answers again later to build your business development component. First, you're starting to build the ideal client: the person you want to get in front of—the person Smiling Sally represents.

Once you've defined your ideal client, you'll talk to people like them to explore the problem you want to solve. Create a list with three columns:

- Column One: The person's name and where they work geographically—these are current or target clients who fit your ideal client profile
- Column Two: What is the emotional issue you are solving for them? (Hint: these are the words you wrote after "because".)
- Column Three: What are the unique skills or attributes that you possess that they truly value?

NAME	VALUE	EXPERTISE

List current clients who you can reach out to and ask questions, clients whose opinion you value and who can give you open, honest, and constructive feedback. Choose a diverse group of clients and build out the list.

If you do not feel comfortable talking with your current clients because of a conflict of interest with the company that employs you, or if you don't have existing clients because you're switching to a different industry, start with some of the potential target clients. There is a wide range of ways you can create this initial list; there is no right or wrong way to go about it.

The best way is usually to find someone who may need your service and start a conversation. State up front what you are doing, and let them know you're only looking for feedback and possibly an introduction to someone else who can help move your thinking forward.

If you are starting from scratch, this can feel a bit clunky, but I promise it's worth the effort to put yourself out there.

In some cases, you may be in a small niche market, and you don't want to let on to potential clients or competitors what you are doing or even thinking about. This shouldn't stop you; I encourage you to consider reaching out to "ideal clients" in a similar market in a different state. There is nothing wrong with making a call and asking someone for a minute of their time. Most will be happy to help.

From there, assess the problem you'll solve for your clients. Delve deep and think like your target client. Often people hear the symptom of the problem they are solving but don't really dig down into defining the real issues.

Just as a therapist digs down to find the core challenges you face, you need to do this with your target clients to be successful. If you can uncover what the real issue is, your research will be much easier and help you identify if you are a good fit for that niche.

As an example, a woman working in a marketing company was interested in being a solopreneur in her own practice. She decided to assess her skills and look at the problems she solved for her existing clients. She knew she was a great technician when it came to creating strategies and implementing social media but realized creating posts was only a symptom of the problem she solved. She thought she provided support to companies by managing their social media content and communication—and she was. Digging deeper, she realized the real problem she solved was removing her clients' fear of looking like idiots online.

Many business owners know they need a social media presence but don't understand the intricacies involved. They are afraid to create accounts, and when they do, they often avoid any engagement. They may not understand the value of being online, they may fear they are missing out, or they may feel nervous having heard about a competitor or friend who got clobbered on social media by not being engaged. They want someone else to cover their social media so they don't make mistakes. Their primary issue is fear.

Through listening, the marketing professional was able to alleviate their fear, step in, and assist, allowing her clients to breathe easy as they knew she had their social media presence covered. She realized she was a strategy expert in the social media market...and she also acted like a therapist by listening and alleviating fear. This is a part of many jobs. An accountant has to deal with the fear their client has over government compliance. A divorce attorney has to work with a client who is devastated at a horrible time in their life.

This social media marketer embraced what she loved and what she was good at. She realized that she was an expert, but she wanted to further define her niche. Her challenge was that there were virtually no barriers to entry in her field. A fifteen-year-old in their basement could conceivably present that they could do the same work, so clients didn't necessarily know what "good" looked like. In order to differentiate herself, she had to think like her clients, embrace her True North, and then she looked at her unique talents and assessed the people on her target list of clients. Who would appreciate her unique skills or assets more than others, and why? Since she had been a veterinary assistant in college and truly loved animals, she was able to speak the veterinary language, understand their concerns, and authentically represent them online. As a result, she was a great fit with small and mid-size veterinarian practices to manage their social media presence.

A PERSONAL EXAMPLE

Growing up, I had challenges with reading and writing letters and numbers out of order. This is most prevalent with numbers, and, as a result, I dislike completing IRS forms—or any government form for that matter—and I stink at completing them accurately. In the past this resulted in some unfortunate letters from the IRS due to late payments. I'm not trying to hide anything, I just detest filling out forms, and I often put important numbers in the wrong order.

My accountant realized that "Hey, this is a smart guy and he gets it, but he is a little afraid, embarrassed, and hates forms. He can tell you the amount in his bank accounts and the performance metrics for his businesses, but filling out compliance-driven paperwork is scary and difficult for him. In his case, his main motivation is fear around screwing something up. And he wants to make sure that I'm keeping him out of trouble."

My accountant understood that I don't need to embrace how debits and credits work. Her job was to make sure my books were accurate, my taxes were paid on time, the companies were in compliance, and that we would both stay out of trouble. I didn't need to be bothered with anything else. Knowing this, she connected me with a great bookkeeper who complements her work as an accountant. This bookkeeper loves and excels at keeping everything organized. She helps to input all the numbers, and my accountant makes sure I stay out of trouble. I look over the books monthly, and if I have questions or something seems off, I ask. But my main concern—almost a phobia—of government forms has been addressed. In this example, both the bookkeeper and accountant have found niches in which they excel. Their work empowers me to focus on areas where I excel. We all win.

She clearly defined the client's problem, aligned with her True North, thought like a client and determined their specific pain point, and determined her unique value proposition.

ASK THE RIGHT QUESTIONS

After you have identified and created your list of target clients, it's time to reach out to them to determine their thoughts and motivations. What specific problem are you solving for them (not the mechanics of what you will do for them, but what root concern are you addressing)? Why would they recommend you to someone else?

I suggest you start this while you are still gainfully employed, but plan on being discreet. Remember that you are likely still gainfully employed and you have not fully decided you are going to jump ship. Discretion will allow you to dig in and learn what you need to learn without raising any red flags to your boss.

Go through the list you created and identify your ideal target client. Reach out to them. If they're existing clients, let them know you want to check in with them and see if you can improve your existing service and would like to ask them some questions. If they're potential clients, introduce yourself and let them know you are researching your industry and would love to get their input. Tell them you want to understand what they like and don't like about their industry.

The questions may look something like this:

- What issue am I really solving for you?
- What do you most value of what I provide?
- What could I do better?
- Why do you like working with me?
- If you recommended me to someone, what would you say to them?
- What frustrates you about our working together?
- What do you love about my industry?
- What do you hate about my industry?
- If you were in my shoes, what would you change?
- What would make you change to a different provider?
- What opportunities do you see for my industry?
- What else do you wish I could do?
- What else should I be asking that I am not?

You must be willing to make the call, old-school style, on the phone. No email. Call them, be honest about what you are doing, and ask if they have a few minutes to talk. Most will, but if they don't, be polite and move on to the next.

A good trick in these conversations is this. If they are willing to speak further—whether they're current or potential clients—use the same questions, but make them generic. Ask about the profession in general, not the specific professional they work with. Give them carte blanche to say exactly what they think about your industry and to offer opinions on how it could be improved. People are often resistant to say something negative about an individual, but they are willing to be candid about an industry. An example may be, "I don't want to talk about my auto repair guy Joe, but let me tell you about how much I hate the auto repair industry as a whole." Those conversations can provide valuable insights.

Remember to *listen twice as much as you talk*. This is why you have two ears and one mouth. It's through these answers that innovation will be found.

The key here is to understand your target clients' *motivations*. I know a high-net-worth financial planner who capitalized on a previous teaching career when he realized that his strongest area of value was his ability to talk to and teach his clients and their children. He realized they worried that their children didn't understand finance and how to manage wealth. The planner said, "I love teaching and helping people." He found a niche not just in managing people's money but also in teaching new generations how to manage money, wealth, and finances. The fear he addressed was the very real fact that most wealth is squandered by the generation following the one that created it. As a result of his work, he empowered the next generation not only to understand how to keep their money and how to work with and understand finances and investing but also how to grow it in a responsible way. The main issue that he defined was the fear of losing wealth, and he addressed this by education of the next generation.

It's through asking questions and assessing motivation that you find a problem that lights you up and that you would love to solve. When you discover the place that gets you excited, it helps you embrace and find the niche where you can thrive.

As you go through each call, take notes. Create a template with the questions you want to ask. Leave some blank lines and fill in the answers for each person. This will be where you start to see trends and possible recurring opportunities.

ASSESS THE MARKET

It's time to clarify your unique value proposition: the points that showcase what you do and how you do it better than others.

You started by determining the specific problem you solve. Now observe how others approach the solution and how easy it is for people to enter the industry and compete.

- How is the problem currently being addressed?
- How can it be done better?
- What would be the ideal way to solve that issue?
- How much are people being compensated?
- What would the ideal solution be worth?
- What skills, passions, equipment, certifications, degrees, and other unique qualifications would help you solve the challenge?
- Is your solution a better, ideal solution than what the market currently offers?
- What is surprising in your research, and how can you capitalize on it? What might you not have considered yet?
- What market challenges did you discover that you hadn't considered?

As you work through these questions, document the answers and begin to think about your offering and how you solve the challenge. I would encourage you to consider how you can research, test, and refine your new ideas while still employed.

A key factor in how the challenge is solved may be related to barriers to entry into the industry. The greater the challenge to enter the industry, the higher these barriers may be and the better you can narrow down your unique value proposition. You often don't know what makes you unique until you list out these barriers, so explore all possible barriers to entry in your particular marketplace.

These can include things like:

- Education
- Experience
- Special equipment
- Unique relationships
- Unique location
- Insurance
- Bonding/Financial guarantee requirements
- Face-to-face interaction
- Large initial capital needs
- Number of people already in the field
- Unique attributes
- Track record
- Security clearance
- Certifications
- License

Understanding these barriers as opportunities can help provide you with a sense of direction. Let's say you are currently an engineer with a specialized background, security clearance, and industry certification. This may offer you an opportunity. I personally have over thirty-five years' experience, a unique (and expensive to earn) strategic planning certification, and am a former business broker; this skillset provides me the opportunity to fill a unique niche.

My wife filled a unique position as a certified English accountant with venture capital experience, but she disliked it. She looked into what it would take to become a counselor. She took time and changed directions to obtain a master's degree, various certifications, and three thousand hours of supervision. These were all barriers to entry, but now she understands accounting, business, business owners, and counseling—which helps her fill a unique niche helping businesspeople with their relationships.

Write out a list of the education, certifications, licenses, and any other experience you have that have been a challenge to obtain or set you apart. Add your innate talent to the list. Look at your life as a whole of experiences and comprehensive body of work. This will be a good starting point in identifying your niche.

....

....

....

....

....

....

....

....

....

....

IDENTIFY YOUR NICHE

Typically, the people who are exceptionally successful are the people who focus on being exceptional at doing fewer things. Success is often found by people who discover a niche. When I advise people in this phase, I get nervous when someone says, "The market is huge, I just need .05 percent to be a millionaire." Great to know, but this tells me this market is likely a commodity-driven business with huge players—they have great economies of scale, and it can be difficult to compete with them. I encourage people to look for the small niche within the market where they can thrive.

Find opportunities that fit with your True North, motivations, and skillset. Find a unique market or even a unique subsection of a larger market, and narrow your focus on that area. These niches are often areas that other organizations aren't paying attention to because they're not big enough for them or are difficult to enter. Once you identify your niche, start to dig in, find where you excel, and focus on becoming exceptional.

If you're an attorney, what is your current niche? Perhaps you work on patents or real estate or business transactions. Find the intersection of what you love to do and where you excel. If you're a counselor, find your specialty. Is it couples and families, drugs or alcohol, sex addiction or faith-based? What aligns with your True North, motivations, and skillset?

Your skillset is extremely important. Don't take who you are and what you can do for granted. Understanding that you have a unique set of skills and what your skillset looks like are basic steps to identifying where you're going to fit. I have a friend who has a very strong faith, and he also happens to be a great architect and researcher. He has experience, understanding, and an expertise that is unique and allows him to build churches. He has the theological understanding and knows the requirements for laying out the physical structure of specific religious buildings.

Every individual has a unique background and set of interests. Narrow your scope by looking back at the problem you help solve. Delve deeper than the mechanics of the job, as those are just responsibilities. A financial planner doesn't only buy and sell stocks; she ensures the safety of somebody's nest egg and helps them prepare their finances for the future.

In some cases, when Reka and I are helping people who are completely lost in their life's direction, we work with them to identify their life-changing goal (LCG). The author Jim Collins refers to this as a "Big Hairy Audacious Goal," or BHAG. Your LCG is huge, far bigger than yourself, and in order to be attainable, it needs to be in alignment with your True North. A great LCG can become the target for where you are going and a way to identify what success looks like on your own terms.

STARTING OVER

If you are sitting there frustrated and saying to yourself, "No, Kris, you don't get it. I HATE what I do, and I want to do something completely different," I promise you—I do get it. In fact, I've started over many times. You may have a longer journey to get where you want to go, but you are on the path. Create a target of where you want to go so you can identify a starting point. If you have no idea, fair enough. Let's figure out the things you do love. Let's go back and look at your motivations and True North. Sometimes, if you don't know where you want to go, the first step might be figuring out where you don't want to go. Your journey may have many twists and turns as you change careers. It will likely require extra research and likely include additional education or training.

If you are lost and want to try it, there is an LCG activity online at aspiringsolopreneur.com that will help you identify your life-changing goal, and from there you can come back here and see if it helps identify your niche and direction.

If you are really stuck, reach out online at aspiringsolopreneur.com for help.

My LCG is to introduce a million people to a different way of thinking and change a hundred thousand lives. My true passion is helping and empowering people to think differently, and I want to have an impact.

The direction you think you're going may change, evolve, and pivot as the idea and research in this process continues. That is all part of the journey—remember you are looking to become the boss now; you can make directional changes as you need to. But you need to be strategic and intentional.

TAKEAWAYS

- Ask yourself what problem you solve. Can it be done better? What are the barriers to entry?
- Reach out to target clients and ask questions to narrow your scope and assess their motivations.
- Define your strengths and unique value proposition—the unique product or service that makes you valuable based on your skillset.

HOMEWORK

1. Document what your ideal client looks like and why they are ideal.
2. Make the phone calls and document the answers to your questions.
3. Document *what* you believe you want to do.
4. Document your barriers to entry.
5. Document the problem you solve and your value proposition.
6. Define and document your unique niche.

CHAPTER THREE

BEGIN BUILDING YOUR ROAD MAP

You were put on this earth to achieve your greatest self, to live out your purpose, and to do it courageously.

STEVE MARABOLI

In chapter two, I encouraged you to identify your unique value proposition and refine how best you can prove your service. You talked to existing and potential target clients to determine their problems and motivations. In this chapter, I encourage you to talk to people who currently work in your field of interest to fully assess the market environment from their viewpoint. Where the last chapter focused on surveying what your potential clients are looking for and what is needed, this next step is to talk to similar businesses and competitors in both your market geography and other locations to learn what you can from those already engaged in a similar business. By surveying the business landscape, you can better define where best you fit.

CREATE A SUCCESS ROAD MAP

The last chapters focused on defining the destination. Now you need to build the road map to get there. This will become the outline you use throughout the entire process, but we're going to start at a high level and then dig into each component over the following chapters. You have already started with the homework you documented in the previous chapters, and now you will build on that foundation.

The road map will highlight the steps needed beginning to end to start your business, define the life cycle of a potential client or customer, and raise any questions you need answered. It will be the place you document all your research, and it will become a forcing device to help you figure out what you don't know. Keep in mind that when you create an initial success road map, it will likely result in many more questions. That's okay. In fact, that is the objective. You want this to be the first step to figuring out what you need to learn and who you should ask. In the next chapter, you'll begin to put together a team of advisors who can answer your questions and help you avoid common pitfalls. In this chapter, you'll develop a list of questions to ask existing businesses. You'll refer to this tool repeatedly to navigate to your destination: solopreneurship.

Remember, you won't have all the answers. The key is to determine the questions to ask and then get those answers in future chapters. At this point, you just have to start figuring out where the gaps are in your knowledge and thinking.

Start by asking some initial questions of each role/hat you'll be wearing. You'll find some of the answers from the previous chapter. The questions for each role may include the following, but don't hesitate to add questions you think of yourself:

INVESTOR HAT

- Is my business idea valid?
- What will it cost to get this business off the ground?
- What financing options are available to get this started?

- What problem am I solving, and how is it currently being done?
- What is my niche?
- What specific product or service will I be delivering?
- How are people currently compensated for this?
- What is the likelihood of success, and will I get my investment back?

MANAGER HAT

- What is the business structure?
- Do I require a business license?
- What taxes do I need to know about?
- Who will do the accounting and bookkeeping?
- What are the legal risks?
- What contracts will I need?
- Are there special insurance needs?
- Where will this business physically occur?
- How will I get clients and drive business?
- Will I be able to manage my time and my focus in multiple roles?

HEAD OF BUSINESS DEVELOPMENT HAT

- Who will value this product or service?
- Why will they value it?
- What makes for a great client?
- What is the life cycle of an ideal potential client?

- Who can I ask for introductions or referrals?
- What will differentiate me from others?
- Where will I find clients?
- What marketing materials will I need to provide?
- How long will it take to close a deal?

TECHNICIAN HAT

- Would I like to work for this new organization?
- Do I think it would be fun?
- Do I need further education and licensure?
- Do I need any certifications?

This road map may be a few pages at the beginning. Going forward, each step will expand to its own section, and in those sections you will start asking questions of industry experts who are potential members of your board of advisors. Also know that the road map will likely never be finished; it's a living document.

At this point you may be panicking. You're in a sweat and thinking, "I can't run to Steve in HR or Tanya in Legal. I don't know where to find this information." You can't just sit with your friend during happy hour sipping a Moscow mule and ask, "Hey, what corporate structure do you think I should use?" Don't freak out. It will be okay! I am going to teach you how to build your board of advisors and answer all these questions.

One of the biggest problems I see solopreneurs face is feeling like they are on an island by themselves. I promise there are others out there you can talk to. Solopreneurs often get together. They discuss ideas and celebrate successes and failures. Virtual peer groups can be found at aspiringsolopreneur.com and can help fill this need. This type of group can help you embrace the journey from being a technician to solopreneur and commiserate with others who are likely experiencing similar challenges and emotions.

FAILURE OF NOT ASKING QUESTIONS

In 1998 I met a construction worker who decided to quit his job and sell hot dogs at a shopping mall food court in downtown Denver. Lunchtime was very busy in the food court and he loved hot dogs, so he invested almost $250,000 in the buildout, equipment, signage, and advertising for this designer stall. He did this without speaking to anyone or considering the costs, and he went all out. He spared no expense with his black and white subway tiles and brand-new equipment. It looked beautiful.

Meanwhile, I owned several coffee shops in the area. I knew the hours of the food court and that the peak times for lunch are 11:00 a.m. to 2:00 p.m. I also could easily calculate that the volume he would need in order to cover his costs was not possible during these limited hours and doing it on his own. He was acting as a solopreneur. It took him roughly ninety seconds to deliver the product to each customer and ring them up. In that ninety seconds, he only netted a gross profit of fifty cents. Out of that fifty cents, that money went to his fixed costs including operating expense and debt, which he was barely denting. He had nothing left to pay himself.

Two months later, he quit. He lost his entire life savings. It sucked, but it happens every day. The moral of the story? He should have vetted his idea and done a financial viability assessment. Another professional would have suggested he calculate the number of customers he would need to serve to break even. He should have looked at his bottom-line profit, not only the top-line gross revenue. In fifteen minutes, he could have vetted his idea and made an educated decision that it was not a good business venture.

This example is depressing, but it doesn't have to be you. You are learning how to avoid this type of mistake; and by the end of the book, you will know how. For now, remember that you have the ability to talk to anybody you want, and you should. The point of building the road map is to ask questions and determine whether your business is viable or whether you need to adjust or pivot to a different direction.

Most people envision business owners as having a yacht

and a private jet. Outside observers are good at calculating the top-line revenue but rarely look at adding up the underlying expenses. Taxes, insurance, cost of goods, professional services, utilities, rent, everything. Ownership often means debt. It means putting your name on the line for any money you borrow. I hate to be the one to say this, but the government typically gets paid first, the bank gets paid second, any employees or contractors get paid third, suppliers get paid fourth, expenses get paid fifth, and then maybe you get some money in the end. Ownership doesn't suddenly mean wealthy.

As you progress through your journey, I will teach you how to build a plan for financial viability. With each step you will identify any costs and make a note, as you will be using this in more detail in future chapters.

BEGIN YOUR OUTREACH

How do you find others in your field and talk to them? In many cases, you can find people right in your own neighborhood or town. Reach out to them and say, "I'm considering getting into the business, and I would love to talk to you. Can I buy you a cup of coffee and ask you some questions? I would love to hear your thoughts, trials, and tribulations."

According to the abundance-scarcity minded philosophy, some people see the glass as half-full, and some see it as half-empty. The more positive person sees the positive opportunities, but the negative person who is more scarcity-minded may refuse to share their information. The last thing they want is more competition or to give away what they consider to be trade secrets. An abundance-minded person will absolutely share with you and answer any questions. "This is wonderful. I would love to have more quality people in the environment. How can I help you?" In my experience, this is, more often than not, the norm, not the exception.

Running a successful business is a victory and an achievement in an owner's life, but they rarely have an opportunity to talk about it. They may or may not share feelings with their partner/spouse, and they certainly don't share feelings with their former co-workers. So when somebody approaches them and says, "Look, I'm considering this, I would love to learn from you and hear your thoughts," more than likely they'll be eager to share their experiences.

If you're playing a longer game and you think that you may not launch your business or practice for another year or two, then you could explore local chapters of professional boards or organizations. Volunteer to be on the board in the area you are looking to launch your business. Even if you are not yet in the industry, you may still be able to join or sit in. You'll be giving your time, but you'll also get to know people in the industry and ask them questions when it feels most comfortable. You may even find new friends and a referral source or two. You will provide valued service in volunteering, and you will gain valuable knowledge without having any financial exposure.

If you're entering a niche market and there aren't many people in your community, or they have a scarcity mindset, you can still find answers elsewhere. We live in a beautiful, abundant environment. You can communicate online with somebody in another state immediately, via video chat or email. Speak to as many people as you can, ideally face-to-face or via video call. Gather as much knowledge as possible so that you can excel in your new roles of investor, manager, and head of business development, not just technician. These interactions will help you begin to connect with others in the community, create long-term relationships, and expand your thinking.

BE PREPARED AND BE GENUINE

When you sit down with someone who's agreed to discuss their business, make sure you are prepared. Show genuine gratitude and express your thanks that they are willing to spend time with you. Pay attention to the clock. Ten minutes before your allotted time ends, tell them so and let them know you want to be mindful of their time. If they want to continue, great; if not, end on time.

Have a list of questions on hand, which may include:

- What do I need to get started?
- If you were in my shoes, what else would you be doing?
- What were the three biggest mistakes you've made?
- What were the three best things you've done?
- If you could go back and do something different, what would you have done?
- What were the surprises?
- What expenses have you seen that you didn't initially anticipate?
- Are you looking for anyone who would be willing to contract?
- Do you know of anybody who's currently looking to contract work out in this field?
- Is owning a business what you expected?
- What is your overhead?
- What do you charge for your service?
- Are you getting what you wanted out of your business now, compared to when you worked for somebody else?
- If you were in my shoes, who would you talk to?
- What has been your best source for business development?

- Who do you use as an accountant, attorney, banker, and insurance expert, and would you introduce me to them?
- Is there anything else I should be asking?

For each of the upcoming chapters, I'm going to ask you to remember to write out your conclusions, additional new questions, and expenses and identify any new insights from the people you talk to: existing business owners, potential clients, and industry experts.

Determine the questions that arise so you can continue to ask better questions and get answers.

The intention with these questions is to learn how these owners address a situation and to learn as much as you can about entering the field. As you go along, you can then get into the mechanics of the business or ask specific questions that you may need to answer to fill in your road map.

GATHER ANSWERS AND PROCESS

The purpose of these meetings and the questions is to learn as much as possible and identify what you *don't* know so you can then educate yourself on those elements. Most entrepreneurs celebrate their failures and are willing to talk about them once they trust you as a fellow entrepreneur yourself. They will often become an open book. Most people genuinely like helping other people, especially someone who shows an interest in their business. They don't want you to make the same mistakes or feel the same pain they did. In many cases, they will be impressed you are taking the time to ask these questions.

Don't stop after the first one or two interviews. Ideally talk with at least three and as many as ten different owners and listen with wholehearted, open-minded, active listening.

As you conduct these interviews, try to observe if these people share your True North and motivations. Let's say you want to get into the car restoration business. Your objective is to restore beautiful museum-quality vehicles. You talk to one car restorer whose business is to restore cars and flip them. In this case, you do similar work, but you don't share the same Truth North and motivations. It doesn't mean his answers aren't valid, but take them with a grain of salt.

As you ask questions of multiple owners, there will be times when two people contradict one another. What do you do? You listen. Don't dismiss either viewpoint; rather, try to actively listen and assess. As you continue to gather answers and build your road map, you will ultimately choose a direction that feels right for you.

LOOK FOR INNOVATION

Innovation and creativity often live in the places that are uncomfortable. When you describe your idea to someone who has a lot of industry experience, they may tell you, "Oh, you can't do that." They may be right. They may be wrong. Remain objective and listen to them because they have the experience, but remember they also have their own insecurities and misconceptions.

Ten years ago, if somebody said, "I'm going to build a company where I will get other people to use their own vehicles to drive people places, and it's going to be worth billions of dollars," people would have laughed. But that's Uber. Uber took a traditional, mundane solution that's been around forever in one form or another and spun the industry around. They found opportunity in the excess capacity associated with people's ability to work on a flex basis, provide transport with their own vehicles, and create a different alternative.

Twenty-five years ago, if somebody said, "You'll be able to purchase anything you want from your recliner at home—from deodorant and toothpicks to cowboy boots and taco shells—and it will be delivered to your front door in two days," people would have laughed. But now we have Amazon. Amazon took on Walmart and Target and helped people save time by delivering products to their door. They created a solution that didn't exist, figured out a way to help people simplify, and as a result went out and did something spectacular.

As a solopreneur, you aren't likely to create Uber or Amazon, but it doesn't mean there aren't opportunities, particularly on the fringes of reworking how something is currently done today. You could have a massive impact on the way something is done, in a way that is very financially successful for you.

So, what can you do? How can you provide a solution in a different way? Write your ideas below.

....

....

....

....

....

EXPLORE ALTERNATIVES

The point of the road map is to outline the steps you will need to take and do an initial assessment. You will begin to smoke out opportunities and challenges that you will face. It's a skeleton; the success guide that you'll create in chapter thirteen will put the meat on the bones. When this is completed and you are finished, it will be your choice if you want to move forward with this version of your business or not.

Sometimes the answers to your questions will lead you to reevaluate your plan. You may interview people and decide you no longer want to implement this idea in its current form. Congratulations! Please celebrate this as a huge victory. Reevaluating your plan doesn't have to signal the end of your dream of solopreneurship; it only means you dodged a bullet on this particular iteration of it, and you now have the opportunity to look for alternatives.

What could those alternatives look like? Perhaps you need to adjust your model and pivot slightly. Maybe the business requires high insurance or an expensive piece of equipment, so your solo practice ends up contracting with somebody who already has those items. You may evaluate one component and decide to contract that part out to another company and adjust your costs accordingly.

You may even decide that a franchise opportunity is worth exploring. Franchises work because a great franchise will take all of these questions off the table. An experienced team has already figured out the answers and put together the brand and marketing. You pay for that in the form of the franchise. It isn't a bad idea, and if it's of interest to you, it may be worth talking to franchisors. Not all franchisors are equal or even are going to be the same price. Some are mature and very empowering and supportive of their franchisees. Others are pretty green and aren't necessarily the most supportive or successful. The initial franchise costs may be less expensive, but the franchisor may have only three or five franchises open and can't offer you the help a seasoned franchise group can. When you buy a franchise, you increase the odds of success, but the franchise does not guarantee it.

If you have chosen to explore alternative business options, I would encourage you to go back and review your motivations. You originally thought you wanted to have your own engineering consulting company, then you realized that a solo venture involves business development, marketing, and accounting, and you think, "I just want to be a technician working for myself." Great. Now you've refined your desires, and your vision has become a little clearer. Rework the road map and start talking to more people. Learn how it works to function as a contractor. Ask, "Do you know anybody who's looking to contract out this sort of work?"

PRO TIP: IS A FRANCHISE A GOOD FIT?

This information is based on an interview with Ryan Zink.

What is the value of being involved in a franchise?

A franchise is a brand and a model that can be dupli-cated. A business owner trades their money and time to be part of this proven concept. As long as they follow the model, they can go out and have success in one of hundreds of industries. There are currently 3,800 franchisors in the United States.

What is the difference between a franchisor and a franchisee?

A franchisor is an organization that is responsible for providing the models. They own the trademark and the brand. They have the operations manual and train the franchisees.

A franchisee is the person who invests into the brand and is willing to follow the requirements. Some fran-chises require that a franchisee be an owner-operator; others allow you to be a manager.

Who is a good fit for a franchise?

I have a franchise scale. If you're a one, two, or three— you are very dependent and need someone to do everything for you. If you're a nine or ten, you are inde-pendent and want things your way. Neither of those are a good fit! In franchising we want the fives to eights. We want the people who are independent enough to make their business successful, but not so independent that it has to be their way.

What are the benefits of going with a franchise?

I believe the stats are 85 percent of franchise businesses are successful, whereas there's only a 25 percent chance of success if you open your own business.

You get a branch, you get a proven operating model, you enroll in training, and you get a network of other franchise like-minded people around you.

How do you know if a franchisor is reputable?

The number one thing a candidate can do is contact the existing franchisees. Call a number of them, have your list of questions together, and continue to call because these people rarely answer or call back right away!

Many times if you can get in early on a franchise, you're going to have more heavy lifting than if you get into a much larger one, but the opportunities are greater. If you wanted to get into a Subway or a McDonald's today, you'd be lucky to find the opportunity to buy one or two. If you wanted to get into some smaller brands, you can open up more locations.

What do franchises cost?

I've seen costs from $100,000 to $1 million to start, and then there are ongoing costs. Franchisors typically charge some type of operational royalty (approximately 5 or 6 percent) and marketing royalty (1 or 2 percent).

What are the top mistakes people make?

The first one is they're underfunded. So many people come into franchising and don't have enough money.

The second is that they aren't prepared for the energy involved to run it. Be prepared!

The third is that they don't do their homework. Make sure that whatever you decide to get into is going to be a good fit.

The objective here is to have a very smooth, safe, and well-educated transition to a thriving solopreneur life. You have yet to quit your job, but you're exploring options, seeing what's out there, and learning what you really want to do.

TAKEAWAYS

- Vet your idea by getting out and talking to people who are doing what you want to be doing.
- Create your initial road map. Each section will contain a space to interview existing business owners, potential clients, and industry experts. Remember to build in any additional questions that come from your owner interviews.
- Begin assessing financial viability. As you go through this process, you're going to be assessing if your business is viable. You want to know start-up costs, monthly costs, how many clients you will need, and how long it will take to earn an income. Document every possible expense as you learn about them.

- Decide whether you want to move forward or consider alternatives.

HOMEWORK

1. Document the answers to the questions you asked both yourself and industry experts. Note any questions you still need answered.
2. Begin to build a list of advisors that you will talk to and the questions you should ask them.

PART TWO

ESTABLISHING YOUR TEAM OF ADVISORS

CHAPTER FOUR

BUILD YOUR TEAM OF ADVISORS

Here lies one who knew how to get around him men who were cleverer than himself.

ANDREW CARNEGIE

You've vetted and refined your idea and begun your road map by leveraging the thoughts and knowledge of potential clients and industry experts. You've added to your list of questions, and now it's time to start getting answers and build out your team of advisors consisting of an accountant, attorney, insurance expert, and banker. They will be a giant help in building out your road map and ensuring a successful transition from your current position in "office hell" to becoming a thriving solopreneur.

Not only can these advisors offer you advice in their areas of expertise but they may also be small business owners themselves. They've been down a similar path, and they likely know others in the field. Not only will you have a team that supports your business endeavors but you'll also be exposed to possible networking opportunities that can further open doors to business relationships and clients.

The goal of building your team of advisors is to be very specific and intentional in your initial questions so that you get the information needed to complete your road map. You don't need to know how to do everything yet; your advisors will help. The information is critical as it helps create future projections of your financial viability, allowing you to mitigate your risk and decide your course of action.

All the sections of your road map will be living documents. I recommend that you approach it with a spirit of curiosity. You don't know what you don't know, and it's critical that you identify potential issues, determine timelines for launch, and assess financial components. Open-ended questions and active listening will lead you in the direction of information and answers, exploration and learning. Every question has the potential to create five new questions, whether for this particular advisor or another on your team.

BEGIN THE SEARCH

You've defined your True North and your motivations. You have begun to outline a path on how to get to your X on your road map, and possibly even a clear LCG. Now it's time to identify the tight curves, roadblocks, and detours between here and there. Talking to business owners, potential clients, and your potential team of advisors will help you determine those obstacles and begin to find ways to avoid or overcome them. When you're looking for members of your team, you need to find professionals who you genuinely trust, believe, and like. Share your True North with them, and look for those who share the same values!

The advice you get by talking to somebody who works at Goldman Sachs could be valuable, but their motivations may be to make a lot of money while yours are to work fewer hours. They may be looking at the financial gain because they have three children in Ivy League colleges, while you want to spend more time with your toddlers. The closer you get to somebody who has a similar True North and motivations, the more likely they will be a good advisor for you.

Advisors may end up being friends, but they're friends you need to trust to tell you the truth, even if that truth is not what you want to hear. Not all experts are the same, so you may end up having to talk to a few to determine the person you want to hire. In the following chapters, I will introduce you to various types of experts and the initial questions to ask. I'll share interviews and advice I've received from my advisors; these are friends of mine and people I admire and trust.

When identifying potential advisors, let them know your planned line of business and that you are exploring becoming a solopreneur. Ask if they work with small businesses in your particular field. Ideally, you will want them to represent at least two other people in that space, as this will let you know they are familiar with your specific industry and any special considerations that may be applicable. If this isn't the case, you can ask them for referrals to someone who might be a better fit. Don't be afraid to ask; remember, they will be working for you.

YOUR ADVISORS WORK FOR YOU

Anyone who is a great small business expert—whether an accountant, attorney, insurance expert, or banker—should be more than happy to give you sixty minutes of their time for free. They should want to invest in you, as that is part of their own business development in an effort to build a long-term relationship.

Always remember, these people work for you. This can require a shift in thinking, especially if you're coming from a blue-collar position and sit down in front of a banker wearing a $3,000 suit. That banker still works for you. You are the interviewer, and if the person acts pretentious, this can signal a personality conflict. Be cautious; you want an advisor you can work with and trust. Shift your thinking from "This guy is an attorney, so he knows everything." to "This guy is an attorney. Does he appear to be the expert I need? Does he want to see me grow? Does he share my True North and motivations?"

You can fire an accountant, attorney, insurance expert, or banker just as easily as you can fire the guy that you hired to mow your lawn. The idea of firing a doctor or an attorney or an accountant can be very, very scary for some, but you have to be willing to do that because your new fiduciary responsibilities are as the owner/investor of your new business. You have to have the best people working with you. If you can't trust them, learn to fire them. There isn't a solopreneur or private professional out there who hasn't been fired at one time or another. That's part of the game. It doesn't mean they're a bad person; it just means they may not be a good fit for you.

Of course, the better process is to spend the time up front to find the right people—both in skillset and a shared True North. Investing this time early will ensure you won't have to fire the wrong person down the line.

Once you've hired your advisors, there are questions that you will be asking to complete your success guide. While each advisor has answers to specific industry questions you're looking to find, there are some general questions you will want to ask each expert. These may include:

- How viable is my plan?
- What do I need to be aware of?
- Who else should I talk to?
- Do you know anyone else in my line of business? Who you can introduce me to?
- If you were in my shoes, would you move forward with this business?
- What else should I be asking?

Note: I realize some of these questions are really vague, and this is on purpose. You don't know what you don't know! You are creating the environment where advisors can provide feedback. You will also have questions you obtained on your initial road map document from speaking with industry experts and clients. Make sure you include those, and then take any questions from each advisor and use them in future interviews! Take notes in the pages allocated for each expert.

....

....

....

....

....

....

....

....

....

If you can get an accountant to say, "You should do this business," you are probably in a financially stable position. If you can get an attorney to say, "You should pull the trigger on this," you probably aren't at risk of getting sued. And you want an insurance professional to say, "You've mitigated a lot of the risk." Don't base your decisions solely on their advice, but know you are definitely moving in the right direction when you can get these answers and map your next steps.

ALWAYS ASK QUESTIONS

You never know where a question will lead you. In one particular case, I helped someone evaluate a vehicle graphics business where he planned to be a local provider for small businesses. He did his initial research, asked questions, and continued to assess his options. At one point an advisor offered him a referral: a real estate franchisee (the individual business owner) that wanted to use vehicle graphics, but their franchisor (the corporate office and issuer of the franchise) was being uncooperative, and they hadn't been able to move forward.

My client agreed to the meeting and reached out to the franchisee, who in turn connected him with the corporate franchisor. The corporate franchisor quickly identified their concerns with the vehicle graphics, that they wouldn't be consistent with their brand across the country in terms of colors and fonts, graphics, and sizes, so they had been resistant to allow their individual franchisees to use them.

My client wanted to become this corporate franchisor's preferred, go-to vendor so that he would be referred to all of the individual franchisees throughout the country as the *approved* vendor. In order to offer consistency, he needed to find a subcontractor for design, another for consistent printing, and then outsource to a national network of professional installers. This road map was different than the one he had at first considered, but within a month of opening his business, he had a corporate account with a national franchise and dozens of individual clients across the country. Going through this process allowed him to continue to ask questions in an area he had limited knowledge of, but had determined there was an established need.

You never know where a conversation will lead, so always be curious, always be questioning, and always be listening. Be receptive to both the good and the bad. You never know where it can lead you.

GETTING YOUR ADVISORS TOGETHER

Why are all of these advisors so important? The one shared interest of this group is the success of your business. Surround yourself with great, trustworthy advisors who are looking for long-term relationships and who can work together with the shared goal of your success. They can also help create the right relationships, offer the right introductions, and smooth out the road so that you can achieve your dream.

Think of your board of advisors as a symphony, and you are the conductor. You don't need to play all the instruments, but you need to know that they are expert players as soloists and that they can play well together. As the conductor you coordinate them, and as a result you all play as a single entity with a shared piece of music. If a musician is off-key, the entire symphony can be ruined. You must trust that everybody's playing their part correctly. The end result is a beautiful piece appreciated by others.

Once you have assembled your advisory team, you may or may not consider meeting with them all together on occasion. Sometimes they will contradict one another, but you ultimately get to make your own decisions. An attorney, for example, might say that you shouldn't do anything outside the box because the likelihood of your getting in trouble increases exponentially. Well, it does. But in some cases, what's the risk of not doing that something? Weigh the risks and make a decision.

Ownership is critical. You need to be able to own your decisions. An employee can blame the boss, or the board, or Tim in HR, or Pam in Legal. When you're the owner, everything stops with you. You have to own your decisions: good, bad, right, wrong, top to bottom. You get to revel in the successes, but you will also need to be wholly accountable for any train wrecks.

In the end you need to realize that you don't know everything, you need to surround yourself with people that you trust, ask more questions, and build from there. Sometimes you will fail, and sometimes things go wrong, but the entire purpose of this book is to help you see the challenges, navigate around them, and arrive. The road map ensures a plan for a smooth transition.

TAKEAWAYS

- You've done the initial assessment and are convinced this is what you want to do. It's time to start fleshing out your road map, adding in notes for the timeline, and calculating financial requirements.
- Part of building a great road map is assembling a great team of advisors.
- Approach it with a spirit of curiosity, and ask a lot of questions.

HOMEWORK

1. Document who you talked to and the questions you asked.
2. Document their answers and the conclusions you reached.
3. Document any new questions you need to ask.

CHAPTER FIVE

FIND YOUR ACCOUNTANT

—

Don't ever let your business get ahead of the financial side of your business. Accounting, accounting, accounting. Know your numbers.

TILMAN J. FERTITTA

All of your advisors are important, but I begin with the accountant because the accountant is the expert who has seen more people financially undressed than anyone. Finding a great small-business accountant has immeasurable value.

My own accountant, Tricia Riggins, CPA and managing partner of RG and Associates, Certified Public Accountants, LLC, actually has an undergraduate degree in psychology and a graduate degree in accounting. She is a trusted friend and advisor who has no problem pushing back and giving me tough advice when necessary. She actually says she views her job as a consultant more than a number cruncher because she helps companies with human resource problems, personnel issues, financial issues, banking, and insurance, working with them to develop a plan to run and grow the company.

Tricia emphasizes the critical importance of locking down your relationship with an accountant as early as possible. This was a universal theme with all the advisors I spoke to; you should involve experts in this infant stage, well before you plan on pulling the trigger on anything—whether it be signing a lease or sending out a contract to that first client—while you are still working for someone else and just starting to think about your solopreneur journey. Remember, at this stage you are still assessing the full viability of your solopreneur option. As good advisors, they will do their best to walk you through every eventuality. Use them as a sounding board. I promise you, quality advisors are immeasurably helpful and you won't feel so alone in this journey.

Note: There are always exceptions to the rule and numbers. If you're going to be running an international business, there could be other areas of compliance and contract negotiation that can increase costs and hours needed. Remember, this is life advice, not legal or tax advice.

AN INTERVIEW WITH TRICIA RIGGINS, CPA

What should someone ask before hiring an accountant?

Ask if they have experience and expertise in your industry. A lot of accountants might just do individual taxes, or business taxes, or might specialize in the medical field, so look for the right person who has the expertise in the area that you're entering. It's also about personality. If you think someone is the smartest person in the world, but you personally don't mesh with them, you're probably not going to use their services or feel comfortable calling when there's a problem. Go to their website and do online research to make sure they've received good reviews from clients. Ask how much they charge up front.

Is the cheapest accountant always the best option?

It's almost never the best option. My firm has moderate prices compared to the larger firms, yet we have all the same expertise. Not all accountants are made equal. Some are experts in generational transactions, whereas others are experts in business acquisitions.

How much does an accountant usually charge?

A bookkeeper will cost about $20–$50 an hour, and the number of hours you use one will depend on the number and complexity of your transactions. A certified public accountant (CPA) bills anywhere from $120 up to $450 or more an hour at the larger firms.

When you first launch your business, the accountant will help with company formation, tax preparation, advisory work, and filing with the government. It's safe to budget approximately $3,000 to $5,000 for the first full year (in 2019 dollars).

What else should someone ask?

If you're starting a business, speak to an accountant about how to form your company. Is this going to be a corporation or a sole proprietorship? I see a lot of people that form LLCs and get taxed as partnerships. They pay way more taxes than they should because they're paying tax on all of their earnings. I've also seen people incorporate and start paying themselves salary when they don't have any net income to actually pay the salary. Talk to a CPA and determine the correct structure for your company. Get that done right at the front end, as it can have lasting effects.

MAKING INTRODUCTIONS

Accountants know everybody! Good ones work with accountants, attorneys, insurance professionals, and bankers, and they likely will be happy to offer you a referral and make an introduction. (If the ones you talk to aren't this connected, they probably aren't a great fit for you or the advisory board you're putting together.)

I once worked with Brad, a financial planner who set up a unique, financially effective, private 401(k) for me. As a trusted financial advisor, he wanted to talk to my trusted accounting advisor to make sure everything was in alignment. These were two areas out of my expertise, so they worked together to create the best plan for me. During the process, Brad and I spent a good amount of time talking about my business, and he expressed an interest in going out on his own and becoming a solopreneur. He had already worked with Tricia, and when she found out he was going out on his own, she expressed interest in using his services. She liked the 401(k) he had structured for me, and she bent over backwards to help him, putting him in contact with three other people interested in signing up for a private assessment. Brad wasn't able to take on new clients immediately, but it was a situation where he was planting seeds for that long game.

I see these kinds of referrals happen all the time. Sometimes the relationship you make will net you referrals from a company who can only handle existing or large clients. I once owned a social media company, and there were times we didn't have the bandwidth or desire to work with much smaller businesses, but I was more than happy to hand those prospects off to solopreneurs I knew. They were technically competitors, but they were doing work I didn't want to do, and I was happy to refer them the work because they did a great job. These are the types of opportunities you want to keep your eyes and ears open for. Maybe you can help with the overflow work from others?

Does it happen every time? No, but it's definitely possible. You have to ask for the referral or introduction, perhaps saying, "Do you know anybody in this space? Do you know anybody who may be looking to contract? Is there anything else out there?"

Down the line when you are ready to pull the trigger, you could already have built a client list, which results in a smoother transition from employee to solopreneur.

FIND THE RIGHT ACCOUNTANT

I hope you've already found a potential accountant or received referrals to several different accountants from the initial discussions with industry professionals back in chapter three. If you don't have someone yet, you can ask colleagues, "Who is your accountant? Do you like them? Would you mind referring and introducing me?" Another option is to go online and check reviews. Call and ask about their experience with small businesses in your area of expertise.

Contact small business accountants, and if you're speaking to the owner, realize they have been down your same path before. Experience is critical, but it has to be the right kind of experience. If you hire someone who is a big-company auditor, they probably aren't a good fit for your one-person business. Just because an accountant knows debits and credits doesn't mean they know anything about small businesses. Having the wrong accountant can be almost as bad as not having an accountant at all.

You also want someone who fits with you and your culture. Tricia's culture is a perfect fit with my company. Her team is great, they bust their asses, have fun, are open and honest, and I trust them implicitly. This is a culture that I share, and therefore, we mesh.

I hired my first accountant when I lived in Colorado, and she was amazing. She worked with hundreds of small businesses and could refer her clients to one another. If she took on a client in a particular field—say, construction—she might have had twenty others in the same field. This was perfect for clients who wanted an accountant who was an expert in their particular field. For the general contractor, this meant she knew the ins and outs of the business, could advise accordingly, and possibly make quality introductions.

I travel on Interstate 80 a fair bit near where I live. I often go through a town where there's a sign on one of the buildings for an accountant. I always thought it was fascinating because this particular accountant is not in an area where there are any offices. It's all industrial and flex spaces. But the sign says, "Trucker CPA," and it is clearly visible from the interstate. That's their specialty. They are CPAs for truckers, and they know their business cold. Their visibility is the ideal spot for them.

It's perfect. If you wanted to be a solopreneur who was in transport, driving a truck, wouldn't you want to talk to an accountant who is the Trucker CPA? Not only do they know your business but they also probably know people who are looking for transport contractors, can give advice about buying equipment, and know your tax write-offs better than anybody else. I don't know anyone there personally, but I love the example.

It's not always easy to find the accountant who's an exact fit for your industry or profession, but I love the idea of a niche because this type of specialization often leads to great matches.

Find the right accountant, somebody you trust, and you may end up making a good friend in the process! Your accountant can almost be a therapist. They are involved in much more than just the debits and credits; they can help you build your business and connect you with the right people, potential clients, and partners.

PARTNER WITH THE GOVERNMENT

A good accountant is going to help you see the government as a *business partner* instead of as an *adversary*. The government has good intentions, but often bad execution. (There's a rumor that as many as 75 percent of letters sent out by the IRS may be sent in error.)

Your accountant is key in making sure that you stay in compliance and your books are clean. They will also do everything they can (within the bounds of the law) to make sure you avoid overpaying taxes. That's the game, and the way that tax laws are structured. Don't try to hide anything. If you have an accountant who suggests that they're going to hide something, run away. Hiding is *very* bad. But you *do* want to write legitimate things off and use "gray" areas. You need to ensure that an accountant is in alignment with your views and your comfort level because some accountants won't write *anything* off, and some accountants will write *everything* off. Find your fit and philosophy.

Follow the government's rules for compliance, fill in forms, and make sure that you pay taxes as, and when, necessary. In some states, if you're late with your sales tax payment, the state has the legal right to chain the doors of your business closed until you pay the tax in full. Remember, you're the one who is ultimately accountable for compliance.

I used to spend a lot of time trying to figure out every little space where I could potentially save money, including loopholes in the tax law. I remember doing a pro forma—a gigantic future prediction on financial spreadsheets on the viability of a real estate project—that I took to Sal, my partner/mentor. He pointed out very gently, but firmly, that it was way too complex. He asked, "What would happen if some of the current government regulations changed, and you were relying on those things?" The reality is, I'd get clobbered. He said, "When you're building financial spreadsheets and looking at the viability of a business, the government is going to be your partner, whether you like it or not. Embrace it. Make sure you factor the cost in, and if the deal still works, it may be viable." These are words I have come to embrace and teach.

The government is going to get paid. Income taxes, sales taxes, licenses, tariffs, and more. If you try to outthink it, you're likely investing too much time trying to game the system. If your business is viable only by playing exclusively in that gray area, then it's probably not a good business. Compliance is key, and changes in compliance rules can dramatically impact your business.

The key thing to note is that working with the system, instead of trying to thwart the system, gives you peace of mind. Your accountant will be a key advisor in government compliance. They will also help you stay calm if you ever do receive an IRS letter. When I get letters from the IRS, I don't worry about them. I quickly open the envelope, take a picture with my phone, and email the picture to Tricia. She will let me know if there's anything more she needs from me.

STAYING ON TOP OF YOUR BOOKS

Part of government compliance means having clean books that are accurate, current, and reflect updated numbers. In addition, this is just good business! The reason for this is that you're going to be required to provide regular reports and filing some of them with the government, your bank, potential investors, and perhaps other entities. The government is not benevolent or willing to listen to excuses, and that is why many solopreneurs hire a bookkeeper.

Some people get confused between the roles of bookkeeper and accountant. An accountant acts in more of an advisory role, is your liaison with the government, and helps with your year-end finances and tax returns. A bookkeeper is someone whose expertise is the day-to-day execution of sending invoices, receiving money, paying the bills, and maintaining records of all financial transactions.

If you are the type of person who loves numbers, and you are very good, and clean, and accurate with them (not like me!)—and if you *want* to do that—then you can consider being your own bookkeeper. There are various online tools like QuickBooks, Quicken, or Peachtree—or you can even use a yellow legal pad or an Excel spreadsheet. The key is to make sure that you consistently show where everything is and has gone. As soon as you fail to declare income and hide money, you may have inadvertently committed fraud, which is bad. Stay away from that.

If you are not completely hardwired to be a great bookkeeper, then you will likely need somebody for a few hours a week or month to help with your bookkeeping. Your accountant can probably recommend a bookkeeper and give you an estimate of how much time and money it will cost. Having crystal clear and clean books is *extremely* important. I find having clean books lets me sleep at night.

If you outsource this task, make sure you review the books on a regular basis so you can get a snapshot of where you are and whether there are any issues or opportunities. You will be prepared to make better business decisions as you start growing your business in the future.

In addition, you're going to want to have checks and balances, which your accountant can recommend. You want at least two people to keep an eye on the books. I actually have three people that see and review my books, in addition to me!

I trust all of them, and they all know each of the others is keeping an eye on the books.

QUESTIONS TO ASK WHEN INTERVIEWING AN ACCOUNTANT

Use these as a reference to start building the accounting section of your road map. Make sure to include any questions you've developed from talking to other business professionals, potential clients, and advisors:

- What type of accounting do you practice? *You are looking for someone who practices general accounting for small businesses.*
- How many of your clients are sole proprietors or solopreneurs?
- How many of your clients are in my industry? *Ideally, you want someone who works with multiple solopreneurs in your industry.*
- What's the average term that you've had your clients? *Obviously, the longer the better!*
- If you were in my shoes, what would you be asking?
- What should I look for in an accountant?
- What do you see as the challenges or pitfalls that I need to avoid?
- How much do you charge?
- What should I budget for accounting fees for my start-up costs and ongoing expenses?
- Do you know anybody in the industry I should talk to?
- Do you know anybody who's looking for more of this type of work that I could talk to?
- Do you know any bookkeepers I should talk to?

- Do you have any bankers or other people that you recommend I speak with?
- What specific issues with government compliance or challenges do I need to be aware of?
- Who else should I talk to?
- What other questions should I be asking?
- (Insert additional questions you've determined you need answered based on your interviews thus far.)

TAKEAWAYS

- Find your accountant early, and make them your trusted advisory partner.
- Accountants are real people and will act as an advisor to help launch your business, help you stay in compliance, and connect you with other potential advisors and potential clients.
- Partner with the government instead of trying to thwart the system.
- Bookkeepers can be helpful for keeping track of your financial transactions and billing.

HOMEWORK

1. Document all your answers to the questions in this chapter to further flesh out your road map.
2. Document financial elements from this section that

will impact your start-up costs and ongoing monthly expenses.

3. Document time elements and constraints that arose out of this section.

CHAPTER SIX

FIND YOUR ATTORNEY

———

Only those who will risk going too far can possibly find out how far one can go.

T. S. ELIOT

As with an accountant, an attorney can end up being a great collaborative partner and sounding board. Your goal is to find someone with the experience working with start-ups but also someone who wants to create a long-term relationship. Some attorneys look at things in a more transactional way and want to quickly move on to the next billable client. This type of attorney isn't necessarily a great fit for the long run.

Seek someone with the right experience, whose beliefs align with yours, who is in it for the long haul, who has a vested interest in your success, and who can be part of your advisory team.

FIND THE RIGHT ATTORNEY

Start with experience and fit. My father is an attorney, and this was very helpful early on. "Thanks, Dad!" Thirty years ago, there were a lot of general practice attorneys, just as there were more general practice physicians. Today, law is a profession where attorneys often invest a lot of time and energy to narrow down their expertise. No single attorney is great at all applications. Some lawyers only practice patent law, or divorce law, or mergers and acquisitions. You will need to invest the time to find the right fit for you.

There are dozens of different types of lawyers, so it's important that you find an attorney who is great at start-up and understands this unique landscape. If your brother happens to be a good divorce attorney, this doesn't suggest he isn't great at that specialty; he just may not have the expertise and knowledge needed to be a great start-up business attorney.

He likely doesn't understand all aspects of the law as a specialist. He may be able to do it, but it may take four times as long for him to complete the needed research or accomplish a task and still not have the depth of expertise.

Look at experience and fit over cost. Even though attorneys are typically compensated on an hourly basis, not all knowledge is the same. By hiring an attorney who specializes in small business and knows your environment, you've chosen someone who already has gone through a pretty hefty learning curve and can likely work through your needs much quicker. Back when I was a business broker, I worked with experienced people who charged twice as much money an hour but could do the work in a third of the time, so it saved my clients money and provided a better service with much more experience and insight.

A good attorney will usually give you thirty to sixty minutes of their time initially to make sure you both are a good fit because they want to build a relationship with you just as much as you want to build one with them. Many attorneys are solo practitioners, or accountable for their "book" of business, even if they are in a large practice; they are often required to bring in new clients and revenue. Keep in mind they aren't just a resource for legal advice; like you, they are building a network. If they are not willing to invest this time, they probably aren't a good fit and they're most likely uninterested in a long-term relationship.

RISK EVALUATION

One role of an attorney is to mitigate your risk. It is their obligation to make you aware of the potential challenges but not necessarily to talk you out of all of them. It is your obligation to listen, weigh your options, and make a decision.

An attorney's job is to help people understand and *be aware* of risks and then mitigate risks through expert advice. An attorney shouldn't necessarily be talking you out of taking any risk. There will always be risk because you can't run a business with zero risk. You're looking for a balance: someone who can explain the risk and advise you. They will point out all the negatives. "You could get burned here." "This could potentially happen there." That's their job. It's up to you to listen, process, and then decide if should you move forward. The decision is ultimately yours to make.

Let's say you're in an industry that requires a high-end piece of equipment that costs approximately $25,000. This could require an agreement and loan structure, and your attorney may chime in and say, "You do realize you're basically going to pay a thousand dollars a month for the next three years, and then it might not be worth anything? Are you sure you want to do this?" I have seen this type of question asked by attorneys and accountants; remember, it is their job to do so.

If you know that this equipment will allow you to bring in revenue of $30,000 a month and you already have a contract lined up, then the answer is an obvious "Yes," but your job is to listen, assess how you would like to handle it, and make a decision.

It is the attorney's job to point out the risk, just like the accountant's job is to point out risk in terms of your government compliance. In some cases, they may try to talk you out of signing a contract or making a purchase. Attorneys are respected, high-status experts in their field, but as a technician you are the expert in yours. By that token, you're on equal ground. You're asking for somebody to *collaborate with you*. Listen, assess, and make your decisions accordingly. Ultimately, you will need to put on your investor or manager hat and make the decision.

WHEN DO YOU NEED AN ATTORNEY?

The small business attorney I work with suggests that there are three main times in particular when an attorney can help you:

- **Start-up:** Advising on the type of structure needed for the business (LLC, sole proprietorship, and so on). You want an attorney who understands your specific goals. Ideally, you would be talking to your accountant, banker, and attorney at the same time because they can all offer suggestions on the most appropriate structure. The attorney can set up the structure for you, but all advisors likely will have opinions.

- **Documents:** Identifying the legal documents needed to be successful. One of your attorney's biggest roles will be in helping you draft and review contracts and agreements. For example, you may need an attorney and insurance professional to review your real estate contract or an operating agreement. In addition, there are documents you will need in order to run the business and documents that you may have to sign to build your business, like a sales contract. This also can apply when purchasing equipment or financing the business.

- **Litigation:** Advising in the instance you are sued or if you are forced to sue someone. If litigation does happen, you need someone firmly in your court— pardon the pun. I believe you should always try to avoid litigation if you can, but the person who doesn't prepare for it and have someone in their corner is the person who gets clobbered and loses a lot of sleep. (Note: if you have a noncompete clause with your current position, make sure an attorney reviews it, as it may result in adjusting your timeline for a start date.)

WHEN IT COMES TO LITIGATION

Determining business structure and drafting contracts are reasons to proactively hire an attorney. Litigation is usually the one time your attorney will be *reactive*.

Unfortunately, we live in a litigious world today. Even if

you're right, it doesn't mean that people can't sue you. It's scary, but that's why you want to have an attorney in your corner. In the unfortunate event that you are faced with a lawsuit, you can turn to someone you trust and can talk to, who can advise you on what some of your best potential outcomes may look like. Even if you're in the right, they may talk you off the ledge and say that buying the SOB off might be your best bet to make it go away. Remember, ultimately, it's your call.

I once had someone tell me, "Some people think that if you're not getting sued, you're not trying hard enough." Some people push the envelope and sue people for anything. I don't believe in that, but you have to be pragmatic. I like to sleep stress-free at night. This stuff weighs on me, and I like to avoid it! This doesn't make me a pushover. I have a good team in place if push comes to shove. Either way, I still sleep well!

People feel very anxious about the prospect of being sued, but it is not as bad as it seems. Nine times out of ten, you will have good insurance and your insurance advisor will have in-house counsel or collaborate with you and your attorney. The only thing you can do is to run your business honorably and have a trustworthy attorney on your side in the event of a lawsuit. Again, I am preparing you for the worst, but in the grand scheme of things, lawsuits are typically rare.

If you are involved in a lawsuit, take a deep breath and ask, "What are we fighting over? What does this really cost? How can I make it go away?" As soon as attorneys get involved, your fees will increase. I've had attorneys in the past who charge me by the minute with a chess clock, so the second my ego got bruised and I started arguing, my fees climbed exponentially. Sometimes the path of least resistance is the best course of action. If somebody gets hurt, or if somebody aggressive brings up a frivolous lawsuit, then settling it to make it go away might be the best decision.

Choose your battles wisely because if you take a lawsuit personally, it can be incredibly draining. I was once sued by a municipality for bad information I had received from a contractor and ended up having to fight with everything I had. The attorneys on their side were salaried for the organization and couldn't have cared less. They just wanted to win. Unfortunately, I took it personally, and it really weighed on me through the multiyear process.

A TEAM OF ATTORNEYS

Not every attorney is an expert in all three instances mentioned. The advisor you pull into your team should be able to direct you to another attorney or be your specific point of contact. Your perfect attorney may not do any of your court work but instead refer you to someone who can create the business structure, another person to draft and review contracts, and a third person in the event of litigation.

Larger firms can be good options because they have depth on their bench in different areas. Smaller firms have limited in-depth experience but can be good as well and are typically cheaper. Sometimes they are solopreneurs themselves and can connect you with other business owners.

There is no right answer, so the biggest key is to find someone who is a great fit with your True North and motivations and has the right experience.

GOING IT ALONE

I don't necessarily recommend this, especially for a first-time solopreneur, but there are online resources and tools to set up a business structure on your own. I have set up at least a dozen corporations on my own online using boilerplate template forms, and it is very affordable; however, the nuances in each municipality and state can change. The potential exposure to litigation can be horrendous.

This isn't a problem if you never have any issues, but if

you do, you want to make sure that things were set up correctly from the beginning. Some people have gone it alone and they've gotten lucky and had no issues. But when you save money early on, that can sometimes mean you did it incorrectly and it can come back to haunt you.

ATTORNEY FEES

I really encourage you to look carefully at an attorney's experience and their particular fit for you *before* you worry about cost. Attorneys are typically compensated on an hourly basis, and not all knowledge is equal. The cost of legal expertise really depends on your industry, where you are located in the country, and if you're working with an individual solo practice or a firm. I've paid as little as $150 per hour and as much as $600 per hour. In some specialized cases I've seen attorneys charge well over $1,000 an hour.

ESTABLISH A LONG-TERM RELATIONSHIP

Remember your True North and motivations, and confirm these are shared with your attorney. You want an expert who you count on to transfer and provide knowledge and wisdom so that you mitigate your risk and stay out of trouble.

AN INTERVIEW WITH ANSHU PASHRICHA

What is your focus?

My legal career has been focused on corporate trans-actions, which involves helping business owners, corporations, and management subsidy corporations with either buying or selling businesses, or otherwise helping document transactions that businesses under-take on a daily basis.

When should a solopreneur start talking to a lawyer?

In an ideal world, you should have a lawyer as a friend, one who is willing to introduce you to the right people. The moment you think of your idea, that's when you talk to the lawyer. Even if your idea has yet to make money, it's worth having an initial consultation with a lawyer who has experience with helping other small business owners.

Develop a concrete plan, work with strategic advisors along the way, and bring in a legal advisor as part of your strategic brain trust.

What questions should the solopreneur ask?

Tell them about your business, what you plan to do, and then ask, "Where do you see potential liabilities? How can I legally limit my liability when I do my business?" Typically, the answer is to form an LLC, occasionally an S Corp, or some other legal entity that provides at least a basic level of legal protection. You will also want to ask about the types of contracts needed to mitigate risk.

The lawyer should want to know what you will be doing. If they don't, I would suggest that you run away. When you hire an attorney, you're paying for their judgment and expertise. Judgment comes from understanding the facts and analyzing them in a certain setting.

A good business lawyer will understand you're just beginning your journey and should help you with two things: determine and put together your business structure and any material contractual arrangements.

Can you explain the difference between a sole proprietorship and an LLC?

They are different in that a sole proprietorship is typically tied to the individual's Social Security number and the income that comes in will be taxed to that individual. An LLC will have its own EIN number and as such will be taxed accordingly. This gives the owner a certain amount of protection from being sued.

After speaking to your accountant and attorney, it may seem that LLCs are taxed very similarly to a sole proprietorship. Frankly, there are a lot of nuanced differences, and that's why you want to speak to a professional.

PRO TIP: ASK FOR A CONTRACT PRICE

An attorney has a fiduciary obligation when they accept a request from you. This means that they will take the time needed to accomplish a task, no matter how long it takes. Instead of giving them an open checkbook and paying an hourly rate, ask what the estimated fees are and then try to get a contract price. For example: if your attorney charges $400 an hour and estimates five hours, offer to pay a contract price of $2,000. They will have to deliver the same quality, even if it runs over the five hours. I often tell the attorney that I started the process myself and only need thirty minutes of their time to give it a once-over. If they say yes, they are now obligated and will thoroughly go through the documentation. It doesn't always work, but it's worth a try!

Additionally, remember that attorneys are human. If it feels as if they're not answering your questions or that you're not getting what you need from them, find somebody else. Trust is key. Don't be afraid to ask questions. If they perceive you as pestering them, they need to embrace that they need to teach you differently or change their methods of explanation. They work for you. The only foolish question is the one not asked.

Look for a long-term business relationship with your attorney because eventually they may know everything about your business: the ins and outs, your goals and intentions, how things started, and where they are going. You won't need them just when you're in trouble but also when you expand and grow or sell. They will be doing a variety of work for you; it can be difficult to disengage later on. If they wrote your original agreement, then they will likely review it for almost nothing. Whereas if you have to move to a different attorney and start over, they'll need to review everything again because they aren't familiar with your company and its history, and this will cost much more. This is why it's key to find someone you trust early on.

QUESTIONS TO ASK WHEN INTERVIEWING AN ATTORNEY

Use these questions as a reference to start building the

attorney section of your road map. Make sure to include any questions you've developed from talking to other business professionals, potential clients, and advisors:

- How many of your clients are sole proprietors or solopreneurs?
- How many of your clients are in my industry?
- If you were in my shoes, what would you be asking?
- What should I look for in an attorney?
- What do you see as the challenges or pitfalls that I need to avoid?
- How much do you charge?
- Do you know anybody in my industry that I should talk to?
- Do you know anybody who is looking for more of this type of work that I could talk to?
- Is there anything that I can do to make this easier for you or your paralegal?
- What structures do you recommend?
- What should I budget for my legal fees for my start-up costs and ongoing expenses?
- What specific issues with government compliance or challenges do I need to be aware of?
- Who else should I talk to?
- What other questions should I be asking?
- (Insert additional questions you've determined you need answered based on your interviews thus far.)

TAKEAWAYS

- Find an attorney who is a good fit and has the right expertise.
- Find an attorney who can help introduce you to other people, is thinking long term, and that wants to see you succeed.
- Find someone who can help advise you or connect you to others on structure, agreements, and potential litigation...whether that is one attorney or three!

HOMEWORK

1. Document all your answers to the questions in this chapter to further flesh out your road map.
2. Document financial expenses from this section that will impact your start-up costs and budget.
3. Document time elements and constraints that arose out of this section.

CHAPTER SEVEN

FIND YOUR INSURANCE EXPERT

Success is having to worry about every damn thing in the world, except money.

JOHNNY CASH

Insurance can be more expensive than most people realize, potentially consuming up to 30 percent of revenue or more when all the types of insurance a business owner needs are taken into account. Of course, the insurance you need depends on the type of business you are in. Insurance costs are something that many solopreneurs don't take into account. Sure, sometimes insurance is just a blip on the radar, but other times it has a major impact. If you're not prepared, you may have to drastically raise your prices to cover your insurance costs. Identifying your insurance requirements can be a key step in determining the financial viability of your solopreneur endeavor.

The challenge is that there are many different types of insurance. As a solopreneur you can choose not to purchase some of these types, but it really takes a trusted advisor to help you figure out the pros, cons, and risks involved.

TYPES OF INSURANCE

All solopreneurs can expect to purchase some type of insurance. Exactly what will depend on the type of business you're getting into and your individual appetite for risk. For example, you may need insurance to replace what you had before as an employee—like auto and health insurance. Perhaps you'll be getting an office or retail space and have to carry specific insurance as a tenant and is defined in your lease. You may need liability insurance if you drive a business vehicle. You may require errors and omissions insurance. The list goes on! And unfortunately, a lack of insurance can present expensive challenges. Here are several types of insurance you may need to carry. Remember, the policies themselves can be very complicated. It's difficult to understand what's covered and not covered in each policy, so having an agent you can trust is important.

ERRORS AND OMISSIONS INSURANCE

We live in a litigious environment where you can be sued

without necessarily having done anything wrong. Also called *professional liability insurance*, this type of insurance typically protects you in the event of an issue that wasn't your fault, or you made an honest mistake. Having a discussion with a professional to see if this applies to you is important.

Most professional service solopreneurs have errors and omissions insurance, and it can help cover when someone goes to sue a solopreneur directly for work they have done. In the event there is a loss, the insurance companies have their own attorneys, and it's not uncommon for them to sue everyone associated with the incident—right or wrong. It seems like insurance company attorneys view their job as a sport. They can sue and be sued by everyone. If you don't have insurance, this legal jousting can be very costly and time-consuming. If you do have insurance, their attorneys will get on the field and bat for you.

In most business environments, errors and omissions is not very expensive unless you've had to make multiple claims or work in a high-risk industry. Ultimately, the decision may come down to what you have to lose. If you're young with student loans and hardly two pennies to your name, suing you won't amount to much of anything, and you may choose, but don't necessarily need, insurance. However, if you own a home, have a 401(k), and have money set aside for your children's college funds, you wouldn't want to risk losing that and will likely invest in insurance.

COMMERCIAL AUTO INSURANCE

If you drive a car for business purposes and are involved in a car accident, technically your business may be held liable because you were driving for a business-related activity. If you are deemed to have been working, the business can be liable for damages related to the accident. Make sure that your auto insurance matches the needs of your business.

GENERAL LIABILITY INSURANCE

General liability insurance typically helps protect in instances of accidents, such as when a customer slips and falls on the premises. Depending on your coverage, this insurance can help cover anything that arises out of the work you do or at your premises that is out of your control. Talk with your insurance agent to clearly define exactly what you're looking for and what you need.

I once owned several storage facilities around the country. I contracted with management companies to manage the facilities. I provided insurance to each individual tenant, but I also had an overarching general liability insurance because strange things tend to happen.

In one instance, a feral cat entered a unit that had been emptied but accidentally left open. The cat then found its way through a tiny opening at the top of a twelve-foot ceiling, entered other units, and caused damage to stored heirloom furniture and the hood of a brand-new car. The insurance covered some, but not all, of the damage, but it's a prime example of the importance of understanding what exactly insurance will cover and having a good relationship with your insurance advisor, as this was for damage that nobody could have predicted. The tenant had renter's insurance, and their insurance company called mine and were able to work it out for the renter. This is a good example of not being able to anticipate all of your insurance needs.

BUSINESS INTERRUPTION INSURANCE

Many people don't take this into account, but you may want to consider business interruption insurance. If you are the family's sole breadwinner, what happens if you get hit by a bus? What happens if you are suddenly disabled? Your clients, the bank, and other institutions may or may not care, but you still may have loans and other payments to make. This insurance can help pay those bills. The types of business interruption insurance can vary from policy to policy, but they are intended to keep you afloat as the sole breadwinner in your family. Like all insurance, you hope you never need it!

WORKER'S COMPENSATION

Worker's compensation is intended to help reimburse an employee for any injury that they sustain during the course of their employment, including any permanent disabilities and lost wages. It can be costly in certain higher-risk industries.

I once knew an entrepreneur, Jonathan, who owned a commercial window-cleaning business. He decided to hire another employee and was required to obtain worker's compensation insurance.

In this particular business, the insurance cost 30 percent of the employee's monthly salary if he only climbed a three-step ladder. If the employee climbed higher than that, the insurance rose to 60–70 percent of his salary. For the taller ladder, if Jonathan paid the employee $25 an hour, he would now have to pay another $18 an hour, for every hour worked, in additional insurance expenses.

Jonathan had to take a step back and assess whether hiring an employee was a good idea or whether it made sense to continue the work himself.

I realize as a solopreneur you will not have employees. In many cases, you may choose to opt out of getting this type of insurance; however, depending on the business structure you set up, you may choose to be an "employee" of the business entity that you establish. As such, you may choose to pay for this type of insurance in the instance you potentially get hurt. Put on your investor and manager hat, talk to an insurance expert, and determine if you need to cover the technician.

HEALTH INSURANCE

Health insurance can be a moving target, especially when self-employed. I have seen my own personal health insurance premium increase by 200 percent in two years and our deductible increase by $5,000 to over $13,000 annually. Covering your own health insurance is difficult but not insurmountable. You will need to factor it into your business expenses and do your research ahead of time before you jump ship. There are counties in some states where you can't even get independent insurance unless you are part of a larger organization, so be sure to investigate what health insurance is available.

As a solopreneur, it's important to be aware of health insurance rules and to stay on top of regulation changes. Communicate with trade associations and ask all of your advisors, "How would you recommend I handle my personal health insurance?" They will likely have suggestions.

Health insurance can often be used as a tax write-off—

meaning you can pay for the insurance as an expense before paying income taxes on that income—but you still need the business to be profitable to pay for it. Cheaper plans make your deductibles extremely high, and you will have to be prepared for that additional expense if you need it. You may be healthy and think that you will never require hospitalization. Great! Stay healthy, but you should still be prepared for the worst.

Don't let this be a limiting factor to considering a solopreneur life. Figure out what it is. It's just an added expense, but it's critical to know how much you need to make to cover it and to build it into your financial liability model.

I've seen too many people worry about their insurance so much they were afraid to move forward. The key is to determine the amounts, build it as an expense, and put it into your plan!

DETERMINE YOUR NECESSARY INSURANCE

Add the best possible insurance person to your advisory team. As with the other experts, when you're on your search for your agent, you will want to ask if they have experience with your industry and have current clients buying this type of coverage. Ask who else you should speak with and what you should be looking out for. Ask if they work with small businesses. They may not, in which

INTERVIEW WITH DAVID BUSHEY, INDEPENDENT INSURANCE AGENT

When should you begin looking for an insurance agent?

I'd say as early as possible, especially if they're going to purchase any equipment or facilities. If you start the relationship way ahead of the game, you can work with your agent to determine the best market for what you're getting into. If you wait until the last second and the bank agrees to loan you money but needs a binder of insurance tomorrow at 4:00 p.m., you'll probably run into problems. If you started months before you're ready to put a deal together, the insurance agent can evaluate all of your insurance needs, the possible markets, and give you indications of premiums so you can put them into your pro forma. You'll be in the driver's seat.

How can an insurance agent act as a business partner?

The insurance agency should be willing to review contracts with you. Whether it's a lease or a new contract for employment, they may have a section where you're agreeing to do something in regard to insurance. You want someone to review that and make sure you're in compliance. This can apply to insurance requirements for triple net leases, vehicle leases, and so on.

If you were a solopreneur evaluating insurance, how would you assess your specific needs?

If I was starting a business and trying to evaluate my risks, I'd start by determining the number one thing that keeps me up at night. Think about the end users of your products or services and what is the worst-case scenario that could happen to one of their businesses or to one of them personally, and then work your way backwards. That gives you a good idea of what's at play. Then talk to an actual experienced agent who has fifty clients in your industry and has seen hundreds of claims in your industry because he can tell you about your blind spots and how to address them.

What are some other types of insurances you've suggested to clients?

- Umbrella insurance. An extra layer of liability insurance over your general liability, auto liability, and worker's compensation insurances.

- Employment practices liability. Everybody should at least review this, as it protects you for claims against the company for discrimination, harassment, wrongful termination, and so on.

- Crime coverage. I've seen a lot of clients that have had employees steal from them, either using payroll or some other means. It's tragic.

- Cyber liability. Not a lot of companies buy it yet, but essentially it's protecting the business owner for claims from clients if there was a breach of their database that allowed the personal information of their clients, vendors, or employees to get out into the public and put them at risk of identity fraud.

case you can ask for a referral to someone who does work with small enterprises. I know a fair number of insurance agents who would prefer not to take certain small businesses on as clients, and that's okay. Make sure to find the right agent who fits with you and shares your values—like every other business advisor on your team.

Most insurance agents are, at the heart of it all, helping people. As you meet with prospective agents, the good ones will know their product and also be focused on business development. They will also likely be great salespeople, which means that they're natural connectors. Ask them who you should be talking to and connecting with.

As you build your advisory team, you will start to understand the components necessary to build and operate your business. Insurance will be a part of the big picture, and you must look at all the applicable costs. Figure out your *need to haves*, *should haves*, and *nice to haves* in terms of coverage for your particular field. *Need to have* could be insurance that the government, a landlord, a leasing agency, or a bank requires of you. *Should have* could be the errors and omissions insurance. *Nice to have* could be the disruption of work insurance mentioned previously.

Insurance agents can be like attorneys in that they've seen everything that can go wrong. Always begin by asking, "What is the minimum coverage that I absolutely must have that is required by law?" If it is required by law, ask what it is and how much it costs. Can you opt out of any of them, and if so, what are the ramifications? You can build from here based on your comfort level and needs.

Having insurance allows you to be proactive. Let's say something bad does happen. Someone suffers an injury and wants to sue you. If you don't have an insurance company to hand it off to, then you *as an individual* are up against a potential barrage of attorneys on retainer who do nothing but fight this all day, every day. If you are properly insured and the situation is covered by your insurance, then the issue is handled between two insurance companies. Two teams of corporate attorneys will talk to each other, they don't take any of it personally, and the issue is settled at the corporate level. In other words, they will likely want to keep you out of it as much as possible. I find this to be a good thing!

Obviously, you always want to avoid using your insurance. You want to run your business as tightly as possible and try to avoid blunders and accidents, but sometimes things just happen. Insurance is one of those things that you never want to use, but you're deeply grateful to have it when you do need it.

QUESTIONS TO ASK WHEN INTERVIEWING AN INSURANCE EXPERT

Use these as a reference to start building the insurance section of your road map. Make sure to include any questions you've developed from talking to other business professionals, potential clients, and advisors:

- How many of your clients are sole proprietors or solopreneurs?
- How many of your clients are in my industry?
- If you were in my shoes, what would you be asking?
- What should I look for in an insurance agent?
- What do you see as the challenges or pitfalls that I need to avoid?
- How do you get paid?
- What should I budget for my insurance fees for my start-up costs and ongoing expenses?
- Do you know anybody in my industry that I should talk to?
- Do you know anybody who's looking for more of this type of work that I could talk to?
- Who else should I talk to?
- What other questions should I be asking?
- (Insert additional questions you've determined you need answered based on your interviews thus far.)

TAKEAWAYS

- Insurance is often a larger component and more expensive than people realize.
- Figure out your *need to have, should have*, and *nice to have* insurance requirements.
- Use your insurance agent as a partner and advisor but also as a *connector*.

HOMEWORK

1. Document all your answers to the questions in this chapter to further flesh out your road map.
2. Document financial expenses from this section that will impact your start-up costs and budget.
3. Document time elements and constraints that arose out of this section.

CHAPTER EIGHT

FIND YOUR BANKER

———

Money can buy you a fine dog, but only love can make him wag his tail.

KINKY FRIEDMAN

We've talked about long-term relationships with all your advisors, but of the entire group, a banker may become the closest to a business partner. Everybody else is typically paid by the hour for their services, whereas a banker generally has a vested interest in your success because they only make money when you're successful. No banker actually wants to take your house if you fail, even if it's listed as collateral. Your banker wants to empower you to be successful.

As with every other advisor, begin looking for a banker six months to a year in advance, before you need anything from them. It's a relationship-driven business; however, not all bankers are the same. Getting to know the right one can be challenging but may be important to the success of your solopreneur endeavor.

USING YOUR BANKER

Your banking relationship is for more than just securing a loan. This is someone who can be a rock star in helping you vet your ideas, make introductions, and act as a partner. You will also likely need the bank's services to accept credit cards, deposit cash, pay vendors, and conduct other types of transactions.

If you think you might need to borrow money once you have identified what you *need* to have, determine if a loan or an operating line of credit is best for you. A line of credit is a note that's available for you to borrow against when you need it, at your discretion. Often, you only pay interest on the amount you borrow, and it can fluctuate, so you might obtain a $50,000 line of credit for your start-up phase, or if your business is seasonal or subject to a slower period, you can use the line of credit to cover expenses during the slower period and then pay off the balance during the active season. Examples may include knowing you need a loan to prepare for inventory for a holiday rush or having a big contract but knowing you're not going to get paid on that contract for ninety days. It is not uncommon to pay it all back and access the line of credit multiple times a year. Having access to cash can be important. A loan is different and provides you all the money up front, and typically you pay it back over a period of time at a defined interest rate for the entire combined amount.

The key is to have these financial conversations early, so the banker knows when and what you'll be looking for and can offer the right solution. Most bankers hate surprises. If you suddenly need money and try to get a loan, they probably won't fund it or they will require a significant amount of collateral, such as your house, your car, or your 401(k). As in the example, if you know you're getting a contract to work for someone, but they won't pay you for several months, you can go to the bank early—perhaps even before you even sign the contract—and let them know it's coming. Then when you have the terms, you can show them the document and arrange for a loan or operating line of credit to use as needed.

In the entrepreneurial world, there is an old adage about bankers that implies they will never lend you money when you actually need it. Only when you don't need it. Having the conversation early helps to avoid this.

BUILD CREDIT HISTORY

If you start an LLC or a subchapter S corporation for your

business entity, you'll receive an employer identification number (EIN) from the IRS. This is typically supplied when you get your legal documentation from your attorney. If you do it yourself, you can apply to the IRS directly.

The EIN acts like a Social Security number for the business. A new EIN is like a newborn baby. Nobody loans money to a one-year-old, and nobody loans money to someone with a new EIN alone. You will need to personally cosign and guarantee for your business entity, which puts your own personal credit (attached to your Social Security number) and personal finances at risk. Eventually, the entity will be able to stand on its own two feet and have its own credit history. Once the business has borrowed and repaid successfully over time, the bank will acknowledge that it is indeed responsible and trustworthy, and you will no longer need to personally cosign or you'll only need to cosign on higher amounts.

SURVIVE A LOAN COMMITTEE

Loan requests are traditionally processed through a bank's loan committee. The bank may have a loan officer whose job is to "stack a file"—create a file of the materials required by the bank for the loan application as well as any governmental compliance. This includes the reason for the loan, the collateral, and everything about its guarantor, information about the prospective borrower, their borrowing track record, contracts in place, and any other necessary forms and documents.

This file is then presented to the loan committee, which usually comprises officers of the bank; they decide if they want to grant the loan. These decisions are based on the assessment, type of loan, whether it fits within their targeted lending parameters, specific loan portfolios, and the likelihood that they will get their money back. Unfortunately, most big banks won't write small loans. It doesn't fit with their target portfolios and loan parameters.

Many bankers will create the file, waste your time, and then say no. The reality is, your loan may not even make it to the committee because the initial banker knew it wouldn't make it through their preliminary qualifications, but they were afraid of being hit up as discriminatory by not taking your file. It simply may mean that your request is outside the parameters of their existing portfolio and what they are looking for, but they often won't tell you that.

If you know an officer at the bank, this can work in your favor as that officer may be able to approach the committee and vouch for you. "I know this person; I know this industry. We've got four other loans in this space. This person seems really sharp, they're doing well, they have a good plan, and they have great credentials; I would recommend we make that loan." The likelihood is higher that you will get the loan, especially if this is with a small community bank where it is easier to create a personal relationship and your loan fits with their portfolio parameters.

Community banks are more likely to take on smaller loans because they're interested in creating long-term relationships with growing businesses. Banking has long been relationship-driven, and it still is. I am very lucky with my banker because she used to own small businesses and understands what it's like to be on both sides of the desk. As you interview potential bankers, make sure you ultimately land with someone you can work with for a long time.

A good banker will ask to see your business plan and want to know about your business idea. They will try to poke holes at your financial viability to see how easily they will get their money back. Don't be discouraged. They aren't trying to insinuate you will fail; they only want to know the probability of success, and you should as well. Showcasing any concerns will benefit you as well. They don't ever want to foreclose on a loan. That's just bad news for them. They want to make sure that the loans they give are successful.

VETTING YOUR IDEAS

The right banker can open all kinds of doors for you. They may know someone who tried what you're trying and perhaps succeeded or failed. When asked, a good banker will offer to make an introduction to experienced people so you can learn from their mistakes or gain tips for success. These can be people who are currently in your business, have been in your business, or even potential clients.

The bank is there to help you make money. It's their entire

motivation! Or more accurately, when you make more, so do they. Their motivation is to help you make money and to make sure they don't lose money in the meantime.

NOT ALL BANKERS ARE EQUAL

Government regulations have had a tremendous impact on banking. For example, it's against the rules for bankers to tell you that they're uninterested in your loan or whether they're uninterested in working with you. The truth is that very few banks are interested in working with smaller businesses and start-ups. This often means you need to find a smaller bank where you can actually get to know your banker and they can get to know you. You want a real partner, and it's crucial to find a banker who agrees and genuinely wants to *be* a partner with you.

PRO TIP: DON'T OVERSHARE

As humans, we often want to show off how great we are, but in the case of obtaining a loan, don't overshare. When it comes to applying for a loan, bankers are very specific in their request for documentation and criteria needed for the loan application. When applying for a loan provide *only* and *exactly* what they ask for in terms of documentation, statements, and numbers. If they need more, they will ask. When you add more elements, the bank is required to consider them, and it gives the banker the opportunity to ask additional questions. In this case, *complete* is better than *more*. This will be a balancing act as your banker shifts to an advisor role.

Different-size banks work with different-size organizations. The big multinational banks will often listen to you because they have to, but the reality is, you won't likely fit their interests, target parameters, or portfolio. They may only want to work with people borrowing $10 million or more. They will be polite and ask you to fill out a bunch of paperwork, but they won't lend you money. You are a new entity starting something from scratch, so if you meet with a potential banker and have the impression they're just being polite, or they keep glancing at their watch while you talk, it's probably not a good fit. They'll never give you a loan because you're a square peg for their round hole.

You might have to interview five to ten bankers before you find the one you want to work with, and I find smaller banks are the best for solopreneurs. This isn't always the case, but it's good to keep your radar up. They typically know a lot of other people in a small community, can facilitate introductions, and are interested in growing a relationship.

FIND THE PERFECT BANKER

When you begin your search and are talking with others in your industry, get recommendations for banks that other small businesses use. Ideally, you're looking for an individual banker who has experience working with

INTERVIEW WITH KATHRYN BARKER, BANKER

Should a solopreneur look for a banker specialized in their industry?

If a banker has a broader background, they can find the right solution for somebody. The more narrow-focused they are, the less likely they are going to be open-minded to other options.

For example, if you were talking to a banker that specializes in real estate lending, they may not think through opportunities to structure credit differently against large equipment because it's not on their radar.

Is it better to go with a smaller bank because you can form a relationship?

Absolutely, yes. One of the important things for customers coming to a bank is the relationship they build with their banker. More importantly, you can gain access to the decision makers at a smaller bank. In a larger institution, you don't. You may have a relationship you build with the banker, but you never really get to meet the people who are part of the loan committee that ultimately have the say.

In many banks, the decision maker may not even be in that community. Then you're totally relying on your banker and their ability to present your credit in the right way. You may be vulnerable to how the bank views that banker.

What are the biggest mistakes you've seen clients make?

Lack of accurate financials. If your financials don't balance, aren't credible nor accurate, red flags will be raised. It's a big mistake that we see all the time.

If we can't believe your financials, then how can we put together a memo or an approval because it's all going to be based on them? And how do we write the story in the right way?

small businesses and maybe even owned their own business. I have several banks I work with, and I like working with small community banks more. The larger banks that hold some of my commercial real estate loans don't even know my name. At the smaller bank, I know the president and vice presidents by name. The vice president and I go to lunch once or twice a quarter. I feel like she likes me, and I like her, and we get along. They are grateful for my business, and your bank should feel the same about you.

As you narrow down your search and begin to interview bankers, the conversation could go a little like this:

"In the near future I may be applying for a loan. I'm not going to do it right now, but I'm looking to create a long-term relationship. Do you fund loans in the $50,000 to $150,000 range?" If they say, "Yes," then great! Ask how many loans they made in the past month in that range, and if they say none, ask about the last year. If it's still none, this person is most likely not the banker for you. They would rather be playing Candy Crush than talking to you. Ask for a referral. "Is there somebody else I should talk to who does work with businesses my size?"

The moral is, you don't want to work with a bank that's just being polite and has zero intention of funding your loan. Nearly thirty years ago, a partner and I started a coffeehouse, Pablo's, in Denver. After I sold my share of the business to my partner, he ultimately was listed by Huffington as one of the top-ten coffeehouses in the country, but the first year we barely had two pennies to rub together.

In our first year we went to a small, local bank. We thought it was a good fit for the coffeehouse, so we walked in and said, "We'd like to talk to somebody about a loan." We sat down with a loan officer, and he literally started laughing at us when we told him our financial position and that we had no collateral. He wouldn't even give us the paperwork to fill out. He laughed at us until we left. That would be illegal today. Many bankers continue to have that mentality about small businesses, but they're more covert and won't laugh in your face. They'll waste your time and then deny your loan.

There are bankers who only do $15-, $20-, or $100-million deals, and they only want to talk to those kinds of clients. I get it now, but I didn't at the time! Learn from my mistakes. It's just part of the game.

START THE SEARCH EARLY

Bankers are the closest thing you have to a business partner. And the biggest thing a banker is looking for is that their money is returned. They're thinking, "If I give this person money, what's the likelihood that I see that money again? Is my investment safe? Will they make the payments?" And it's literally that simple. When you come in and present yourself as an engaged, knowledgeable, *proactive* partner with a clear plan, it helps that banker tremendously in regard to lending you their money.

You've already begun this journey as you outline the financial viability with each chapter. It will become a part of your success guide, and an accountant can help you create this document as well. This is where you have crossover with your team members. The financial viability will help you identify the costs involved to start and run your business, and this will help you determine the likelihood for success.

The main motivation for an accountant is to keep your books clean and keep you out of trouble with the government. The main motivation for an attorney is to keep you out of trouble and keep themselves out of trouble. The main motivation for a banker is to help you make more money and that they don't lose any money.

QUESTIONS TO ASK WHEN INTERVIEWING A BANKER

Use these as a reference to start building the banker section of your road map. Make sure to include any questions you've developed from talking to other business professionals, potential clients, and advisors:

- How many of your clients are sole proprietors or solopreneurs?
- How many of your clients are in my industry?
- How many business loans of my size have you made in the last year?
- If you were in my shoes, what would you be asking?
- What should I look for in a banker?
- Do you offer lines of credit?
- Do you offer Home Equity Lines of Credit (HELOCs)?
- How best can I build credit for my new entity?
- What do you see as the challenges or pitfalls that I need to avoid?
- Do you know anybody in my industry that I should talk to?
- Do you know anybody who's looking for more of this type of work that I could talk to?
- What specific issues with government compliance or challenges do I need to be aware of?
- Who else should I talk to?
- (Insert additional questions you've determined you need answered based on your interviews thus far.)

TAKEAWAYS

- Your banker can—and should—be your partner.
- Not all bankers are equal.
- Talk to your banker *before* you need money.

HOMEWORK

1. Document all your answers to the questions in this chapter to further flesh out your road map.

2. Document financial expenses from this section that will impact your start-up costs and budget.

3. Document time elements and constraints that arose out of this section.

CHAPTER NINE

ALTERNATIVES TO BANKS

———

I view investors as our partners and stakeholders in the company. They are trying to build financial models. What I try to focus on is helping them understand how we think.

RUTH PORAT

We've talked about the importance of working with a banker and aligning with someone who will ultimately think like a business partner. They will help you vet your ideas, make introductions, and help with collecting money and processing payments. But when you initially start out, a bank may not be the place where you first obtain financial assistance, no matter what kind of relationship you have with your banker.

In fact, starting out, it may be difficult to get a bank loan. They require a great business plan, the right experience, established collateral, plus a variety of other conditions you must meet before most bankers will approve any kind of loan.

So, if the bank won't provide you with a loan, how *do* you finance your business? There are several alternatives.

FINANCING OPTIONS

As a solopreneur, it's imperative to define the funding you need to have. If you're entering business with a low financial barrier, you don't need much capital to get started, but there may be a lot of people doing what you're doing. If you're entering a business with a high financial barrier, you will likely need to invest a lot of capital. This could involve purchasing specialty equipment or investing in an expensive physical location. Other barriers may require capital to pursue a certification or unique licensure. The certification may be a differentiator that helps you succeed, provided you have the capital to invest the time to obtain these specialty items.

Most likely you will be somewhere in the middle. This will force you to narrow down your scope and establish what you really need. You'll have to analyze each purchase before breaking out your cash. When starting to figure out your initial start-up financial requirements, the easiest way to start is by identifying the *need to haves*, *should haves*, and *nice to haves*.

Need to haves could be insurance, your legal structure, baseline marketing components, and baseline equipment. In other words, you absolutely need to have these items to open the business. *Should haves* could include an office location instead of meeting in a coffeehouse or marketing collateral you can use to help close a sale. *Nice to haves* could be an espresso machine, promotional equipment, and a larger marketing budget.

As you work through your success guide, you will begin to unearth these different items. Once you've listed them, you can review them to determine what will provide the most impact for the capital invested. Go through these following sections to compile data in order to make an educated decision. Through this process, you will compile all the elements into your financial viability plan. When you start to consider investing personal money or borrowed money, things will start to become real!

Once you begin to clarify what you really *need to have*, you will be able to determine how much money it will take to launch. Then, if needed, you can review alternative financing options to a bank loan, which may include the following:

YOUR OWN SAVINGS

Start with the cost of the *need to haves* and evaluate the

funds available from a personal perspective, beginning in your own pocket. Your personal capital may be your best resource because it took you time and effort to obtain it and you may be a little more cautious and careful with those funds. Perhaps you have savings you can use, or you can borrow against your assets, house, 401(k), or other investments.

When looking at your savings, note that in most cases this is all after tax dollars. In other words, you have already paid taxes on this money. If you're loaning it to the business entity, you should set up a formal financial note—a loan document that you may make from your new entity to yourself. The IRS may want to see this document, and your attorney can assist you in creating it. Include the loan amount, interest rate, duration of loan, and consequences of not paying it back. Regardless of the source, use a note whenever you borrow or lend the entity money.

CREDIT CARDS

Sometimes solopreneurs pay for items on their credit cards, but it's important to take into consideration the high compounding interest rates. I once started a business in the 1990s by putting $60,000 on a credit card, which was huge back then. It was all the money I had. The interest rate was terrible, it wasn't smart of me, and I

PRO TIP: DON'T COMINGLE FUNDS

A reminder, this is not legal advice; this is just from my personal experience. In most cases, solopreneurs set up LLCs or subchapter S corporations that they work within because they are looking to separate their personal and business liabilities and assets. This works, but make sure you follow the rules that your accountant advises. One of the rules is not to comingle your business and personal funds. Commingling of funds means that you're using business funds for personal usage and sometimes vice versa.

If you buy home groceries and then office equipment on the same credit card, you need to make sure you pay for the office equipment, and share of the interest, from business funds and you pay for the groceries from personal funds. If you pay off the entire amount with business funds, you may technically be comingling funds. I keep it simple and use a separate credit card for each business that I own as well as a different credit card for personal use.

Business expenses need to be legitimate business expenses. You can't use corporate funds for personal use. This tends to happen a lot as a solopreneur. As an investor in your business, you need to keep an eye on it. You wouldn't allow comingling as an investor in a major company.

Not only is this the right way to handle finances but it can also help you maintain the veracity of the corporate veil. The primary reason that most companies set up an LLC that is run as a corporation is so they have corporate protection between them as an individual and the company. In the event of a lawsuit, typically the suing entity will go after the organization first. If that entity gets sued, in a perfect world the most that can be received is the asset value of that entity, not the personal assets of the individual.

However, if you have been using the business for personal expenses and comingling funds, a good attorney can pierce that corporate veil and say, "Look, the corporation only existed for protection purposes. They still made personal purchases with the business funds." As a result, they may now have access to not just the corporate assets but also your individual assets.

This is a really rough, high-level explanation! Don't take this for gospel. If you have any questions on this—contact your attorney.

don't recommend that anyone do the same! It worked out in the end, but I had many sleepless nights and succeeded despite myself. It was foolish.

Most who put money on credit cards roll the dice, hope for the best, and often fail. They shift their balance from one card to a new one that has a zero percent interest rate for six or twelve months. This is a shell game and has questionable fraud concerns that can eventually come back to haunt you. And if the business doesn't work, you could become an indentured servant to the debt for a very long time.

Remember, this is one of the main reasons you are doing this entire process: to make sure you are going into this venture with your eyes wide open and with a clear plan for success. Being clear now will help you to avoid these possible money traps in the future.

HELOC

Using credit cards can be risky. Other options include borrowing against or liquidating your 401(k) or obtaining a home equity line of credit (HELOC) against your home. Make sure this is a collaborative effort you discuss with your partner/spouse before pursuing these options. There are significant ramifications to your credit if you don't repay any of these debts.

HELOCs can be the cheapest, easiest, most effective source of borrowed money for the average solopreneur start-up. The bank uses your home as collateral, but they do require a personal guarantee. If possible, I typically suggest this option before using cash because the cash can remain as a backup and the interest rate is often better than a bank loan since it's collateralized against your home. The caveat on this is that you have to have the discipline to ensure that it gets paid off as you do with any borrowed money. If you don't have the discipline, I urge caution. Once the equity in your home is gone, it can be difficult to see it again.

That being said, if the arbitrage—the difference between the rate at which you can borrow money and the interest you can make from it—is not much between the HELOC and a bank loan, and if you have a good relationship with your banker, take the loan from the bank. This helps you establish that long-term borrowing relationship with the bank and will create more long-term opportunities.

If you're only going to borrow money once to start and keep your head above water for the first six months—for an education, certifications, or straight launch—you may be better off using some of the equity in your home via a HELOC.

LEASING AND CORPORATE CREDIT

If your business requires equipment, computers, or vehicles, you can explore leasing or a credit option offered by the supplier. Most companies will have internal leasing agreements, work with leasing associations, or have internal or external credit options. It's not uncommon that this may cost more, but again you can write the expense off as a deduction against pre-taxed income of the business.

If you need a specific piece of equipment, go to the distributor of the equipment and ask, "What sort of funding sources do you have for this equipment?" I built coffeehouses in the 1990s, and the suppliers for espresso machines and refrigeration were more than happy to coordinate corporate credit to further their sales. This is not always the best financial option because the interest rates can be really high, but it could work for you.

Their job is to make it easier for other people to buy equipment. However, just because the equipment is available, it's important to assess if you really need it. Could you purchase used equipment? Can you sublease or rent part time similar equipment from someone else? Is there another way to do this? Or do I need this latest and greatest widget? Sometimes you do, and sometimes you don't. This is where you assess your *need to haves*, *should haves*, and *nice to haves*.

Typically, leasing rates are much more expensive because of a higher risk. This doesn't mean it's not an option, just that you must fully understand the lease rates and calculate the total liability costs. Refer back to The Rule of 72. If somebody charges you a 36 percent interest rate, you will pay twice as much in two years. The advertising world has done an amazing job in having us focused only on monthly payments instead of the total obligation on the balance sheet. This doesn't mean you can't move forward, but you must evaluate the expenses and be financially savvy. Consult with your accountant if you're unsure how to calculate the total obligation. Decide if this expense is a *need to have*, *should have*, or *nice to have*. You have a fiduciary obligation to this solopreneur business you are investing in.

FAMILY AND FRIENDS

Some people choose to borrow from friends and family. Be cautious since this option is not without consequences. If you do so, your relationship dynamic can change dramatically and quickly.

Make sure that everyone plays nice. Use an attorney to create a very specific, legal, binding loan document (note) so that both parties clearly understand the loan and expectations. Address the terms, when you will pay back the loan, expectations for inspecting the financial books, and what the recourse is for nonpayment. Do this before the funds are dispersed; if in the future you do need to review the document, you will want to know that it was created at a time when everybody was in a positive frame of mind. Have a hard conversation about worst-case scenarios. Be open and honest.

If you borrow from family or a partner, they may feel entitled to get involved in your business and offer opinions. They may feel the right to question your motivations. They may ask to see your financial books. They may question why you aren't working on a Tuesday when you are at your child's soccer game. They may ask why you have a new car but haven't yet paid them back. Understand that you have control over their money, and you may have to explain some decisions along the way. If you're taking a lot of free time or suddenly have a new car, it is possible they're going to turn into Joe Pesci from *Goodfellas* and want their money back! This could restrict your True North and motivations, so it's critical to manage expectations up front. Talk it through and make sure they understand the full story.

FINANCIAL PARTNER

Financial partners can come in a variety of forms. It could be a financial partner is an individual who believes in you and your idea and is happy to own a part of the business or give you a loan at a little higher interest rate. It could be a business that wants to offer you a loan to help you get started, then contract with you in exchange for a discounted rate going forward for your time. There are a variety of options for these loans, but make sure you understand lender expectations and set up legally binding loan documents. Keep in mind that some lenders may want ownership interest in your business in addition to interest back on their loan. If faced with this, you will have to decide if it is worth it to you, and that involves a much larger assessment.

With financial partners, it's important that you create a form of accountability, communication, and expectations early on in the process. This should include your expectations of what they are contributing in terms of funds—and their expectations of you in terms of time, deliverables, and repayment plans. Taking other people's money can sometimes come with major ramifications. This is why finding alternative lending solutions may be preferable.

PAYMENT IN ADVANCE

Early on, you may target client accounts and contracts that people may be willing to pay you in advance. This can be another option to set you up for funding your launch. If you plan to be a specialized contractor for a larger firm, you might be able to ask for the first three months of payments in advance for a 10 percent discount, discounted office space, or some other variation. The negotiation options are unlimited!

Don't be afraid to ask questions or negotiate, because you never know where opportunities may arise. In some cases, that department that you're contracting with may have money in the budget that they need to spend before the end of the year. That's a good quid pro quo for both you and the department. You have cash up front in the form of a retainer to work in advance, and they have allocated their budget the way they want going forward. Again, create legally binding contracts early so you can control expectations.

MAKE YOURSELF JUMP THROUGH HOOPS

No matter which financing alternative—or likely a combination of alternatives—you use to borrow money, it's important that you put on your investor hat and make yourself jump through hoops before spending the borrowed funds; otherwise, it's easy to blow through it all.

First, make sure your business is financially viable and that it is clear you know specifically where the money is going. You're basically "playing bank" for yourself, and you need to itemize and detail how you will spend the money. Put your investor hat on and ask yourself, "Do I really need this? What am I specifically using it for? Is there anything else that would be cheaper and more efficient? Will this make enough money so that I can pay my loan back?"

QUESTIONS TO ASK YOURSELF

Here are questions to ask yourself that allow you to think and act like a banker:

- If I loan my entity the money, what's the likelihood I'll see this back? Think like an investor.
- Is there an alternate way of funding what I really need?
- Have I reached out to my suppliers?
- Have I reached out to my potential contracts for advance payment?
- Did I look for a used piece of equipment?
- I'm buying a truck, and Ford Motor Company will loan me money. Is this the best way to do this?
- Are these tools that I need, and what's the likelihood that I'm going to get paid back?
- Am I in alignment with my relationship partner on this?

TAKEAWAYS

- There are several financing alternatives to banks.
- Solopreneurs should only start with *need to haves* and try to avoid borrowing from outside.
- Solopreneurs may consider negotiating with target clients and distributors/suppliers.

HOMEWORK

1. Document all your answers to the questions in this chapter to further flesh out your road map.
2. Document financial expenses from this section that will impact your start-up costs and budget.
3. Document time elements and constraints that arose out of this section.

PART THREE

PREP FOR LAUNCH

CHAPTER TEN

DEFINING WHAT YOU NEED IN A SPACE

———

Oh, the places you'll go!

DR. SEUSS

I suggest moving slowly and with caution when it comes to real estate. Ask your advisors for their opinion on real estate. How important is the space? Are there alternatives? Do they know anyone you could sublease from? Explore all options and assess your *need to haves*, *should haves*, and *nice to haves*. Is this something you need from an image perspective in order to meet clients, or can you use somebody else's location? Can you dedicate a room in your home for an office, or do you need to work somewhere where there is equipment? Can you lease or borrow space?

I have seen business owners make more massive mistakes in the area of real estate than any other area. They decide to launch a business, sign a lease for three years at $2,500 a month, and are suddenly $90,000 in the hole for a liability before they even open their doors. They were initially unsure if they even needed the space. They weren't wearing their investor hat—they went right to what they wanted and weren't looking at it from a financial perspective and *need to have* basis.

ASSESS SPACE REQUIREMENTS

It's important to identify your specific office needs by asking yourself several questions:

- Do I truly need a space?
- If so, when will I need it?
- Am I certain I can afford it?
- What will I use it for?
- In the interim, what's the minimum amount of space necessary?
- Why do I want it? Is it something I need to have, or is it mostly serving my ego?
- What other alternatives are available?
- What is the monthly rent?
- Is there someplace I can borrow space?
- Do I know any strategic partners who have space I could sublease?

Consider what you need, and test it first. You may find a place you can rent for a few hours a week and then build from there. Avoid initially purchasing real estate unless your career as a solopreneur is as a real estate investor and you're purchasing a place that you know as a real estate expert is a great deal. Avoid signing a long-term lease as well when you are just starting out.

FROM HOME OFFICES TO HOT BUNKING

Start with assessing your needs and motivation for wanting a workspace. Once you know those, you can assess the market. There are many different solutions for the solopreneur who doesn't need a set workspace with equipment. There are specific short-term setups throughout the country that are perfect for solopreneurs!

HOME OFFICE

Often, a solopreneur can start by working from home. You can get away with doing almost everything virtually, especially in today's world!

While I think it's a great option for many, you will need to be completely pragmatic about the type of person you are and if you are suited to working well from a home office.

When you're at home and at your home office, just

because you need to change that light bulb or take out the trash doesn't mean you should at that time. You need to stay focused, work to set hours, and take a scheduled break if needed. Know that you're creating a new habit and need to stick with it. It's easy to get sidetracked and start working on a honey-do list. It's at times like this where you need to act as a manager. Your technician role needs a manager, not a janitor. By taking this approach, you will start to hold yourself accountable and stay focused.

I promise that most people who transition to a home office first think, "Wow, this is going to be great." It is great, but it can be very quiet, lonely, and difficult to stay focused on work.

If you do start at home, create an actual office with a door that allows you to "go to" work and "leave" work, even if your "commute" is thirty seconds long. Visually and mentally prepare so the moment you walk through that door you are *at work*. Focus as if this was a real office. It now is. Other people in your household need to understand that when the door is closed, you are working and can't be bothered. This is a two-way street—you can't go chat with them in the kitchen and watch Netflix during your work hours.

If you don't have a specific room to use when working,

designate the kitchen or dining table as your office for specific work hours during the day.

For the first sixty to ninety days, work a regular routine. Decide your working hours, and stick to them. Dress professionally because there is a professional, accountable attitude that the majority of people adopt when they are in different types of clothes. You are the manager and need to act professionally. If you want to wear a suit and slippers, fair enough! But it's important during this initial time to get into a habit and set this discipline from the get-go. You are now accountable to yourself—which means that if you're late, nobody will give you a hard time. If you don't get your work done, nobody will give you a hard time or a paycheck. If the business fails…nobody will give you a hard time. Act like the manager and hold yourself accountable.

This is the time you set your boundaries—in terms of yourself, your family, and your potential clients and customers. Some people don't want clients coming to their home, whereas others don't mind. If you want to explore this option, you may want to look into any government zoning regulations for business use. This should be easy, and you can get feedback or direction from your accountant. Also talk to your partner/spouse to ensure everyone is on the same page and agrees with the plan and direction.

COLLABORATIVE/SHARED SPACE

If you feel that you're experiencing a bit of cabin fever or want to meet with clients face-to-face outside your home, then you might consider a collaborative or shared space where other people work. This option is growing nationwide and can be ideal for a solopreneur.

Collaborative spaces can be giant bullpens or large office spaces with many small, independent offices. They typically have conference rooms and a reception area, and you can rent a cubicle or a desk in a bullpen area. The challenge in a shared space is how easy it is to chat with others and for others to come talk to you. Establish parameters around privacy, and be firm about keeping them. Perhaps you let the group know that when your light is on, you can't be bothered. It's work time, and you need to have your head down and focus on work.

You may pay a higher per-square-footage cost for rent, and you may have to chip in for the coffee machine and administrative needs, but you only have to use it when you need to. Typically, the lease terms are flexible, which is one of the greatest benefits.

OFFICE SUITE

Another alternative to a home office is an office suite, which is very similar to the collaborative space. There are a variety of office suite environments and options available across the country and the world. Some are their own offices, while others are part of a larger, subdivided office space. In some cases, you can rent by the hour or lease a permanent office month to month. You may or may not have shared conference rooms, conference centers, or a shared kitchen. Some have a shared front desk, administrative assistance, and the ability to receive documents and packages. Shared office suites are typically rented on a per-square-foot basis, and the time frames can be from hourly to monthly. They may be much more expensive than collaborative space. The rule of thumb is that the nicer the location and amenities, the higher the expense. But it may offer some flexibility and be a good way to start. Often these may have agreements with sister locations in other cities. If your solopreneur model involves travel, this may be good option to consider.

HOT BUNK

The Hot Bunk is a term I like to use that I believe originated in the military when ships in the Pacific were so booked with personnel that they had to take turns sharing bunks. You didn't have your own bed, but you had one available from hour X to hour Y. The same holds true for some office space options. I've seen couples' counselors, accountants, consultants, and other professionals use this idea of shared offices. I have seen this in practice with designated days or hours that each person can have as their time to use the space. This can be a great option if you start moonlighting from the beginning. In other words, while still gainfully employed, you may be able to sublease someone else's office in the evening, weekends, or other available time slots.

JOINT VENTURE

You can also explore a joint venture or using another professional's excess capacity. Excess capacity is extra capacity that is not currently being used. Uber and Airbnb have found ways to use that excess capacity model for vehicles and real estate in a way that allows the owner to make additional revenue. In this case, there may be a business that is in a period of growth or decline and happens to have more office space than they need. They may have no problem generating additional revenue and renting it out for a shorter than normal lease period. Some companies will do this with just their conference room or office space or both. If this may fit for you, remember to ask your advisors if they know of anyone who may have space you can use.

Connect with an existing business—and potentially clients—with extra office space, and ask if you can rent their conference room or a portion of their office during the times you will be working. The purpose here is to avoid a long-term commitment but get you out of your house to work somewhere you can focus without distractions. This type of space places you in a professional environment and provides a professional setting where you can meet clients. I have known many solopreneurs who used this model when getting started.

I also know solopreneurs who contract to do business with other businesses in their industry and rent out a small space in their retail location. I knew a jeweler a long time ago who owned his equipment and worked out of his home. As he looked to expand his clientele, he made an arrangement to rent a tiny corner office within a jewelry store. This was mutually beneficial as the jeweler had a larger, public workspace and a built-in client base. The jewelry store owner received value because he had an onsite jeweler who could make repairs, giving customers an added reason to come into his store.

I know engineers, designers, therapists, financial planners, and a variety of solopreneurs who have found value in this option.

COMPARING OPTIONS

There are many options available, and it's up to each individual solopreneur to define their needs. What works for one person may not work for another. It's up to you to define this, but I consistently believe that anything with a long-term agreement is probably not the best solution when you are just starting out. When in doubt, I would urge people to err on the side of simpler and a shorter term when they are first starting their business.

Without knowing your situation and what's available for you, it's hard to say what's best. However, often the best office space for starting your solopreneur business is to rent from somebody with excess-capacity space, even though you may have to accommodate their whims.

Next, I would consider alternative spaces, flex spaces, and short-term leases. They are usually higher in square-footage cost, so this option may not seem cost-effective for when you're starting out. However, by not having a long-term lease, these options are often smarter choices in their flexibility and short-term usage. From there consider collaborative spaces, but be aware of the possible challenges of the work environment. Again, they are often a good alternative because they are short-term.

Some people want to buy their own building. I don't have an issue with that, but the timing needs to be right. When you are getting started, your finances might be tight, and it is okay to rent. You can use that time to determine your exact needs in terms of a future space and location. You are starting a business; the last thing you need is additional stress or becoming a property manager on top of everything else. The goal here is to stay focused on the important elements.

Once you have launched, stabilized, and feel like you are starting to thrive, then you can go out and look for long-term office solutions. When you have achieved this, you will then know what you really want and need in a great workspace.

THE TRUE COSTS

If you decide to sign a lease, have your attorney review the terms before you sign a lease. Leasing a business space is typically far more complex than renting an apartment, maybe even than buying a home. It's important to take the time to assess the true costs because even with renting, some people fail to think about all the long-term factors.

I see it all the time. Someone says, "We only pay three thousand dollars a month for our space," which sounds great until I delve deeper.

- If you're looking at renting in a defined office suite, you'll want to understand the additional services and fees. Ask how much it costs to rent the conference room, how much you pay for paper copies, how much it costs to have someone answer the phone, and so on. (Yes, some places will charge you per page copied, minute of conference time, and guests received...and that's okay, as long as you walk in with your eyes wide open.)
- Build-outs can be required for some new office or retail space that needs construction before the doors open. That extra cost has to be added in. In this example, let's say it's $20,000 for extra build-outs, permits, carpet, walls, and lights. This may not even include furniture, fixtures, and office equipment (FF&E).

- Common area maintenance (CAM) charges may not be included in the monthly rent. If that's the case, factor in your share of the building's monthly expenses, as you may owe a portion each month. Common area maintenance can include items like trash, snow removal, cleaners, toilet paper, coffee, kitchen space, and so on. This can be hundreds of dollars a month or more.

- Triple net leases dictate that you're responsible for your portion of the CAM and often your share of the taxes, your share of the insurance, and your share of utilities. In some cases, you may be liable if the air conditioner dies, the furnace goes out, or the parking lot needs to be redone. Long-term leases can make you responsible for many extra costs, so be fully aware and prepared. Have your attorney and insurance agent review the proposed lease.

- Once you have your extra costs, take a look at the length of your lease and total cost. A five-year-lease at $3,000 a month plus the $20,000 build-out means you're on the hook for $200,000 before you've even opened your doors. These are long-term liabilities and things you have to pay back, regardless of whether your idea crashes or succeeds.

- The investor in you should shudder at the mere thought you've just committed to $200,000 before you make a penny of income! Ask yourself if this is the best way to do this or if can you get around it. Think of your office space needs with *need to haves,* *should haves,* and *nice to haves* in mind.

CONTEXT AND LOCATION

Context is important. If you're starting a legal or accountancy practice, or offering financial advice, it's important to project the image of a trusted and trustworthy professional. Meeting at a coffeehouse or at your house may not communicate that message. You don't need a corner office in the most expensive office building in town, but you do need to meet clients in a professional setting.

If you're in the counseling field and will work with Medicare and Medicaid clients, consider a convenient location near your target market rather than a high-end location. If you're an architect, consider trying to sublease space from one of your main target clients, such as an engineer. Locate yourself near, or with, your clients or near businesses that share your client base. Remember the old truism of real estate: location, location, location. I would always prefer to have an okay building in a great location rather than a great building in a terrible location.

Have a pragmatic debate with yourself on what you really need. Understand that you may go through two or three locations before you finally get that dream location. If you visualized a nice corner office in a skyscraper, and that's where you see yourself, that's wonderful, but it doesn't mean you'll start there. That thinking gets people into a massive lease and a balance sheet that's $100,000 or more in the negative with the stroke of a pen.

I'm not saying you can't get there. If that's a goal or a motivation of yours, you can end up there in the next year or two. But start off by really assessing what you need in terms of location and space based on what is important to your client, not to you.

DO YOU NEED A REALTOR?

Realtors are not always necessary to the solopreneur business, but if you plan to own or lease space, good realtors can be important when it comes to finding great properties. Be your own advocate, however, and do not use a realtor who wants to charge you for showing you properties. Most realtors get paid when the contract is signed, and as such they may not be concerned whether it's a good or bad deal for you.

Keep in mind that realtors also don't always play nice with other realtors. They may like to only show you places that directly benefit themselves, not necessarily everything on the market. In their little world, there isn't anything else. They aren't usually compensated well for renting places represented by other firms, so they are less likely to show you, the renter, all of the available options. They would rather earn the commission by showing you properties they work with and only those properties.

You can do a lot of the legwork on your own. Hop on Craigslist or search for spaces online. Get in your car or ride your bicycle around areas that interest you and look for signs. Go back to the business owners you've spoken with in your industry and ask if they know of any available space or what they think are the best locations.

Once you find a location—with or without a Realtor—consider bringing in a trusted advisor or savvy friend to get feedback on your space decisions. Ask them to help you evaluate how you're spending your money; ask them if it makes sense and if you're being responsible.

This holds true with every major business decision you make. What do you really need? What's going to matter to the client, not to you?

TAKEAWAYS

- Think about your motivations and what you really need in terms of office space.
- Consider a home space, but also address boundaries and set a schedule for the first sixty to ninety days.
- Consider alternative spaces/options.

HOMEWORK

1. Document all your answers to the questions in this chapter to further flesh out your road map.
2. Document financial expenses from this section that will impact your start-up costs and budget.
3. Document time elements and constraints that arose out of this section.

CHAPTER ELEVEN

MARKETING AND BUSINESS DEVELOPMENT

———

Half the money I spend on advertising is wasted; the trouble is I don't know which half.

JOHN WANAMAKER

Marketing is the process of getting your name out there and introducing people to who you are and what you do. Sales and business development involve marketing, but the focus is on engaging with potential clients, growing the business, and closing sales. Some people confuse marketing and business development, but combined they cover all aspects of thought leadership, logos, collateral materials, case studies, networking, social media, strategic partnerships, and alliances. There are dozens of great books focused on helping you with any and all of these aspects.

As a solopreneur you *may* start with marketing to introduce your business to potential clients, but you *must* focus on the business development aspect of acquiring and maintaining your clients.

In my experience, most businesses overestimate the importance of marketing and underestimate business development when they first start. Most marketing is a *nice to have* rather than a *need to have*. Clients are the *need to have*. Because of that, marketing only provides value if it's actually opening doors and driving your business.

THE RIGHT MARKETING LEADS TO SALES

With marketing, you want to get your business name and service in front of the people who are going to value your product or service. The right marketing will drive the right clientele. Depending on the situation, some of your best marketing may be to attend networking events, or to speak with people directly on the phone or in person. Whatever endeavors you proceed with, make sure you spend your time, energy, and focus asking, "What do I need to do to drive sales?" If in the beginning you can drive sales by engaging people in conversation, I consider that a form of marketing and business development.

It's easy to become overexcited about the wrong marketing. Many solopreneurs get wrapped around the axle creating a logo, letterhead, and a great website before they're even clear on what their clients want. This is often insecurity or ego-based, and instead they could have gone online, purchased a good quality logo for $300, and made a hundred phone calls in the same time they wasted on a logo. This is a prime example of needing to put on your manager hat and block out your time to focus on what you need to do first and foremost. You need to define the activities that give you the most bang for your time/buck and drive business development.

Unfortunately, when you're starting off in marketing, you have to acknowledge that *you don't know what you don't know yet*, and your task here is to *ask questions and listen to the answers*. A mistake that I often see first timers make in their initial messaging is that people like to tell a customer all the features and benefits they offer rather than actually focusing on *the problem that you're solving*. When marketing, it's best to define and address the pain someone is feeling before you tell them how you will go about solving that pain.

SCRATCHING A SPECIFIC ITCH

So where do you start? Unlike finding your financial, legal, insurance, and banking advisors, it can be very difficult to find a trusted advisor for marketing or business development. I would urge you to look at it this way: you already have more than one marketing advisor—your ideal potential clients.

You defined your ideal client, your value proposition, and your niche in chapter two. You know the product or service that will scratch a consumer itch. Your marketing has to answer the question "What exact itch am I scratching?" The answer to that question drives an effective marketing plan that allows you to get your message in front of new target clients.

A silly analogy I use with some of my younger clients when talking about features and benefits is this: Imagine you are single and sitting at a bar, and you see someone across the way. You get a wink and a smile in your direction. You walk over and offer to buy that person a drink. You sit down and begin to talk about yourself, your new Tesla, how you won your tennis match that morning, and your daughter just won the spelling bee—without ever asking the other person a single question about themselves. You do a great job of telling all your features and benefits, but it may have nothing to do with what that person wants. Good luck, I don't think that is going to work out how you hoped!

Now imagine you walk over, sit down, and you ask that person about their life, their thoughts, their dreams, and their day. You actively listen, make eye contact, and really try to learn about them. You ask about work, what makes them happy, and what activities they enjoy. You *identify their needs*. As such, you are far more likely to know how to sell your features and assets in a way that benefits them based on this listening and the intel you received. You can now turn around and talk to them about the things you know they will value. You're now able to relate the features and benefits to the exact need they want to fill.

Often, technicians list all their degrees and certifications on their marketing collateral, which testify to their knowledge of their *how*. That's great, if potential customers are looking for those specific items, but those items are really a baseline. Are you going to hire an accountant who is not a CPA? Are you going to hire an attorney who is not really an attorney? These are the bare minimum requirements. You want to get past the minimum. You need to clearly understand the problem you're solving and discover *what* they need so you help them define *why* they can trust you to solve it.

Refer to your road map and everything you know about your ideal customer, their needs, and how your value proposition solves their problems. This knowledge empowers you to design a marketing plan that will drive your business development based on your clients' needs. Remember to go back to your previous work in chapter two and find any additional questions that are appropriate to ask potential clients to learn about their pain and needs.

OFFER FREE ASSESSMENTS

Not sure what your clients want? Don't be afraid to offer a free one-hour assessment. You already learned the value of this from the time your advisors have given you. An hour gives you the opportunity to do the following: actively listen, identify what they need, see if you want to work with the client, show how you can help them, and then provide the next steps for what an engagement would look like.

Once you have established rapport, ask your clients and potential clients the same types of questions that you asked your advisors back in previous chapters. "Hey, Joe, tell me where you got information on my services. Where are places you've seen similar marketing? Where do you seek out further information on these services? What sparks your interest?" It's easy to assume online marketing is the only marketing that exists. You may be surprised by the places your clients learn about your type of services; it may be from direct mail or attending a convention. This information helps you decide where to do your marketing.

Don't think of this as giving an hour away. I would encourage you to think of it as an hour investing in understanding your market, learning what someone really needs, creating a new long-term relationship, and potentially landing a new client.

This combination of marketing and business development direction will help to identify your initial marketing plan and where to invest your time. Your primary objective is to determine what people need, who you need to get in front of, what they value, and where will you find them. You need to determine which fish want the bait you have, what lake they swim in, and then go fish there!

The more you communicate and listen to customers, the more you will understand that you are scratching a particular itch for a laser-focused niche. You learn the exact problem to solve, and at that point you can begin advertising and marketing to a very specific group of people with a much higher likelihood of success. Narrowing the scope allows you to save time, money, and materials.

During the first six to twelve months of preliminary research—remember, in many cases you are still only doing research and have not pulled the trigger yet—you're clearly defining what you need to do, where you're going, what works, and what doesn't. You're doing market research to figure out exactly what people want and value. You are not a marketing expert, although it's imperative that you become one. And in order to do that, spend the necessary time to learn *what people want*, *what they value*, and *what's important to them.*

BASIC MARKETING/SALES REQUIREMENTS

Don't try to figure out your brand without knowing your audience first. Quickly come up with a basic name and logo, purchase the domain, and set up a website. Spend an hour or two on the logo. Anything more than that is likely better spent making calls with people who can result in real-life sales. You can always rework and improve your logo in the future if needed. (The exception to this is if your business is creating logos, in which case your logo had better be damn good!) Once you have a first draft, ask potential clients for feedback and get their thoughts; use it as an excuse to get in front of them.

If you're a tech company or plan to conduct all your business online, you should invest in a decent website. Don't make it over the top. Include basic messaging, contact information, and anything necessary to display your competency. *Less is always more*, but that bare minimum needs to be high quality.

Once you've determined your audience—what they want and where they live—you can move into marketing and advertising. I consider advertising to be a potential part of marketing. If you are a professional, LinkedIn ads may be a great place to start for your industry. These ads can be very focused and specific. If you plan on going to traditional networking functions, trade shows, and trade associations where you meet people face-to-face, you may need business cards. If you don't like to attend these functions, if your target clients don't attend these functions, or if your industry doesn't use cards, don't waste time or money purchasing them. Remember to fish where the fish are.

WORK WITHIN YOUR BUDGET

The simplest, and I believe most effective, way to market and develop your business is simply finding a way to get yourself in front of the right people and start talking to them. Once you have a small client base and you've determined the itch you're scratching, you can begin to build a business development budget. Start by looking at your cost of acquisition, which is the amount spent in marketing and business development dollars to bring in a new client, and the lifetime value of a client. Don't limit your ideas to traditional advertising. Maybe your target clients happen to be members of the same country club, and so the cost of acquisition of three new clients would be worth a membership to that same club.

I knew an attorney who chose to leave his large firm and

create his own private practice in general law. He knew he had to figure out where the clients he wanted hung out. It seemed that most of them played golf, and he liked to golf, so he decided to join a country club and play three times a week with people he didn't know. He would call the pro shop and say, "I'm a single and I'm looking to join a twosome or threesome." Once they got on the course, he now had three full hours to simply chat with two or three other golfers in a stress-free, recreational environment. He didn't sell them; rather, he got to know them. Eventually, they would ask what he did for a living and a conversation would result. He built his entire practice within a couple of years. He probably had business cards for marketing, but he didn't even need a website. In this particular solopreneur's case, his marketing requirements were very simple and effective.

START SMALL WITH SOCIAL MEDIA

I used to own a company that handled content marketing and managed daily social media for clients from New York City to Indonesia. I had a wealth of writers, social managers, and strategists on staff. Based on this expertise, I would advise most solopreneurs that if your target market is on social media, focus on one or two platforms only and do them extremely well. Avoid the rest, and by avoid, I mean don't even create an account! It's easy to set up Instagram, Pinterest, Twitter, Facebook, and LinkedIn accounts and then do nothing with them. This can be counterproductive and can possibly harm your business if you're not staying on top of social media engagement and complaints. Whatever you start with, you must stay consistently engaged and have a business-focused strategy.

If you naturally love Twitter, spend time on Twitter. If you happen to enjoy connecting with people on LinkedIn, spend a little time to learn it well and use it. If you sell a visual product, join Instagram and Pinterest. As with all marketing, meet your clients where they spend their time—online and off. Realistically, are you going to sell specially subcontracted engineering on Facebook or Pinterest? Probably not. It's important that you know your tribe, where they live, and what matters to them. If you aren't on a particular platform, there's a good chance potential clients aren't either. But if you sell jewelry online, absolutely set up an Etsy account and use Pinterest and Instagram to showcase your images and influencers wearing your products.

BUILD A COMMUNITY

It's important to begin reaching out and building your network and your community from the early stages. Staying top of mind is one of the reasons I send out a weekly blog post and a weekly newsletter. It's a weekly tap on the shoulder to remind somebody, "Oh, yeah, that's what

Kris does. He helped me with that." Remember to always include a call to action to encourage further interaction. "Call Now For..."

A mortgage broker I know found it highly effective to mail out postcards each month. They were printed with sporting-event calendars, seasonal tips, recipes, and were the kind of thing you might think would be frequently thrown away. A lot of them were tossed, but a lot of them

PRO TIP: STAY ON TOP OF YOUR ACCOUNTS

Like I mentioned, you need to stay on top of every social media account you create. Early on, this is an area where I was clobbered myself. Your business and reputation can suffer if you don't check pages and accounts regularly and respond to them.

Schedule an hour bimonthly in your calendar to check social platforms. People do read online reviews, and you don't want a negative comment to sit like a red flag, driving away business. Search your name on Google at least once a month to see if reviews have been written about you. If they are positive, use them in your marketing! If they are negative, make sure to address them. In many cases you can't change any comments, but you can ask your tribe and existing clients to go out and provide positive feedback or comments that will push a negative comment further down the list.

You can also balance or bury bad reviews by asking clients to post positive reviews. There's nothing wrong with sending a steady, happy client a link and making that request.

were tacked on clients' refrigerators so that everyone who came over saw them.

The postcard served as a constant tap on the shoulder that this person was a trusted advisor who had provided their mortgage, and when they needed a new mortgage, or someone asked for a referral for a mortgage professional, that's most likely the person they contacted first. People can forget who helped them with a professional service, but they are reminded with newsletters, postcards, LinkedIn posts, Facebook posts, and so on.

THOUGHT LEADERSHIP

If you are in an industry where you are unique in your thought leadership and this thinking will be valued by others, having quality content can be a differentiator. Thought leadership involves two components: you have to have something to say and you have to have a network to say it to.

For example, I keep a list of potential blog topics to write that are pertinent and of value to my audience. I write them and distribute them to my audience via a weekly email newsletter, on LinkedIn, and across my social media accounts. (When I say "I," I have contracted with a rock-star person who cascades out the messaging and monitors my accounts.) The information is broadcast to my followers, and hopefully they choose to share the content. Ideally, the combined body of work ends up creating value for people, showing me as an expert in my space and helping to keep the services I offer top of mind.

START TO NETWORK

Networking is key for getting referrals and finding potential clients. Before heading to a networking event, develop your elevator pitch. "Elevator pitch" is standard nomenclature for the briefest description possible of what itch you scratch and how you do it. Imagine you get in an elevator with a potential client at the lobby level, and you have their undivided attention for thirty seconds. The pitch does *not* list your features and benefits but *does* briefly and succinctly explain how your product or service will help. Here is mine:

> I help entrepreneurs be successful, get everything they ever dreamed out of their business, and safely launch their solo careers.

In the ideal elevator pitch, you address the product or service you're providing *and* the itch you're scratching. The goal is to get someone to ask, "How do you do that?" followed by, "How much does it cost?" Now you're making a relationship that could become a sale.

The elevator pitch needs to be genuine, from your heart, and easy enough to remember. It may be clunky at first, but when you go to pitch someone, it has to roll off your tongue. It has to come from your soul. You have to believe it and know it in your heart. Practice it until it feels natural. As you repeat, practice, and refine it, the pitch will finally become seamless. When you feel the pitch inside and out, people will see it as authentic.

The real key to becoming great with an elevator pitch is to have it come from the heart—and then practice, practice, practice. It will make a difference.

JOIN A BOARD

I encourage you to consider joining an industry or professional board of directors, and you can absolutely do this before you launch your solo business. Joining boards allows you to meet others already in the field who likely own their own small business. You will build a network and begin to create your group of advisors. You will also discover what's already working in your field, what is not, and what has yet to be discovered. These positions offer you the opportunity to showcase your professionalism and individuality.

Virtually every professional community has a trade association board. Volunteer to be on that board, potentially as treasurer or secretary. (Most people hate these positions, and you will be a hero for taking one on!) Find something that fits your personality or skillset. You may take on something you know you need to improve on and see if the current seat can help you do that and get trained. As part of serving on the board, you'll learn about the issues, opportunities, and challenges of the industry.

It goes without saying, but show up early and do a great job. Show that you're reliable and trustworthy. These people may end up being referral sources, whether for creating your business plan; looking for office space; or introductions to insurance agents, bankers, or even clients. You can't know where these contacts may pop up again when you're running your business. In a professional environment, everything you do serves as marketing for your own individual brand.

Joining and working on a trade association board, or in some other associated professional community, can be a productive use of your time in terms of marketing. Similarly, national or international boards may be well worth your time and energy. Attend those, but make sure you are prepared to do the work and to talk to people often. These events are where a ton of professional-service business gets done.

As you meet people in your industry, you'll discover what works for them in terms of marketing. I suggest a little R&D, but it's even deeper than that. Take time to investigate the *good* job that others are doing, and then you do it in a way that makes it *great*. The process helps you focus on your specific value proposition and define what you're doing really well.

GIVE AND RECEIVE REFERRALS

I believe for most solopreneurs, the number one source of any new business will be direct word-of-mouth referrals from other people.

Word-of-mouth marketing tactics are highly worth your time during this early period and potentially your entire career. You don't need to buy billboards or a Super Bowl commercial. The cornerstone of any word-of-mouth campaign is to do great work. Sometimes the best marketing we can do is done by providing a great product or service to our client.

As mentioned repeatedly, ask for referrals from trusted advisors. They'll be key players in getting people to talk about you and your business via word-of-mouth marketing. In most cases, this is the most effective way to market and grow your business. Some studies suggest 85 percent of us trust the opinions of people we know, so be your own advocate. Lean on your advisory board to introduce you to people, and with any luck, you'll have a new referral source.

Word-of-mouth marketing doesn't take a big budget and allows you to test and try anywhere. Here, I say, *Done is better than perfect*. You want to start to identify your exact target market, and the more you narrow that market, the better. You're trying to pinpoint two things: *where* they are and *what* they value. By trying a couple of different marketing techniques, you can figure out what works, refine it, and build from there.

Remember, the goal with any marketing is to close deals. You're not Coca Cola and trying to build brand awareness with the entire world. You're trying to make your niche community aware and then drive sales.

As you begin to network, and even in the beginning of your journey when you are assessing your niche, get in the habit of asking clients and colleagues for referrals. Some people fear asking for a referral because they don't want to appear rude or pushy. The reality is, if you're doing great work, people will want to help you. If they are a connector and believe in what you do, it will make them feel good to help you solve your problems.

This is often a two-way street. When you find people you like and trust, begin to ask them what their ideal client looks like and offer referrals as well.

"Connectors" are important in your role as a solopreneur. A great connector is a person with these three identifiers: they genuinely like you personally and would be a quality connector for you, they believe and trust in what you do, and they genuinely enjoy connecting people. Not everybody is hardwired to be a connector, but those who are can be invaluable allies. Sometimes people feel bad asking, "Hey, can you connect me with someone?" But a true connector—if they like you and believe in what you're doing—receives value by making the connection because it makes them look great. Don't be afraid. Ask, "Do you know anybody else that I should talk to?" Your client may not have someone. It's okay if they don't. Or they may say, "Now that I think about it, yes! Two of my friends."

For each referral, suggest that the client or colleague do the introduction. Ask how they will do the connection, when they will make it, and can you follow up? Get specific. Make sure you know the date, time, and expectations. I like to suggest they connect us via an introductory email. I then ask when they plan to send the email so I can make sure to respond on time. Finally, I ask if there is anything I can do to help.

When mutual friends or associates vet you and vouch for you, clients are naturally more welcoming. As a whole, people tend to make decisions based on the opinions of the people they know and trust. It's a vote of confidence for one side and a solid reference on the other side. The connector enjoys their role in the middle, and as long as they're going to look good for making the introduction, they love connecting people. You empower them to help solve a problem. If you tell a connector you will do something, or if they do connect you, you must make it your number one priority to follow through and do what you said you would. You can only embarrass a connector once. If you embarrass them by not responding, they will never refer someone to you again.

TAKEAWAYS

- Take time for market research and determining the most effective way to get in front of your ideal clients.

- Implement marketing efforts that make sense and work within your budget.
- Make sure your marketing is focused on the itch you're scratching. Business development is what really matters!
- Network and ask for referrals.

HOMEWORK

1. Document all your answers to the questions in this chapter to further flesh out your road map.
2. Document financial expenses from this section that will impact your start-up costs and budget.
3. Document time elements and constraints that arose out of this section.

CHAPTER TWELVE

MAKE SURE YOU'RE GOVERNMENT-COMPLIANT

———

Real integrity is doing the right thing, knowing that nobody's going to know whether you did it or not.

OPRAH WINFREY

We are fortunate to live in the most abundant and opportune environment possible to start a business...possibly ever. I believe we live in the most amazing country, with the most well-intentioned government ever. The government is helpful in many situations; however, the government is not benevolent. It is often a giant collection agency and bureaucracy that does not care about you. It will shut your business down without a second thought. For all the good that comes from the government, it is my opinion that, unfortunately, government regulation and bureaucracy is one of the biggest killers of small business.

New solopreneurs often don't take into account how much it costs to stay in compliance with government standards and requirements. It's understandable. Just because you're great at sales doesn't mean you're great at paying your taxes or filling out the potential plethora of applicable forms. You are likely coming from an organization that had an entire team of people that focused solely on compliance. You now have to become that team.

Not understanding government requirements is, unfortunately, not an excuse in the government's eyes for being out of compliance. Managing and maintaining government compliance is *extremely* important and an area where many solopreneurs get in trouble. As you interview each of your advisors, ask about compliance across all government agencies in the areas of labor, environment, income, safety, and anything else that may be unique to your industry. Also ask about requirements that need to be followed according to municipal, state, and any special district codes. Make a list in your road map and factor the cost of compliance into your financial viability. Begin to add compliance dates to your timeline and in a special section on compliance in your binder.

I've seen a multitude of businesses get clobbered as a result of noncompliance. It is *very* important to stay in front of compliance issues for your business area. In fact, it's safe to say that *the biggest issues I've had in my business*

career have been with the government, and not with clients.
Even when I thought I was doing everything right, I still
ended up having challenges.

Note: Don't panic. This information sounds drastic, and
it's very important, but when you stay in compliance all
will be fine. Everyone has the classic nightmare where
you'll wind up in jail because you accidentally messed
up your taxes. This doesn't happen. Don't freak out! That
said, take this seriously and don't hide anything. If you
don't think you can make money while being aboveboard
with the government, then it's important for you to consider reworking your model to see if it's actually viable.
You may have to consider a different business opportunity.

BE AWARE

Government compliance touches many different aspects
of businesses. For example, a mortgage broker living in a
town that sits on the border of two states may need to be
compliant with two different sets of state regulations on
funding loans or even advertising. This can be impacted
by something as simple as where a newspaper containing
their ad is distributed.

The possible concerns are endless:

 • Renovating a building requires submitting requests,

studies, and other paperwork. This can take up to a year before receiving construction permits. These holding costs have to be taken into consideration.

- Running a business from home and receiving clients there may lead to a fine if the location is not zoned for commercial usage and you frustrate the neighbors.
- Failing to pay sales tax as a result of an honest error may result in the government closing operations or seizing assets.
- Making sure you have the right types of licensure and certifications.
- Making sure you are compliant if you are selling or shipping a product across state or international borders.
- Making sure you are compliant if you are providing a service across state or international borders.
- Being aware which taxes you are liable for, which could include sales, income, property, state, federal, and special taxes.

It's entirely your responsibility to make yourself aware of the regulations that affect your business. Going in with the intention of running your business aboveboard and having advisors to help you do the best you can is important.

DON'T TAKE IT PERSONALLY

The previous section represents the negatives surrounding compliance. Take this to heart, but don't let it drive you. Once you know the pitfalls, they are usually easy to avoid. If you do get thrown a curveball, remember that for the most part, the government doesn't take anything personally. Everybody's blood goes cold when they see the return address on an IRS envelope, but I discussed in chapter five that up to 75 percent of IRS notices may be sent out in error, and they don't really seem to care.

If and when you encounter an issue—whether it be a compliance issue, a tax audit, or an issue related to your location—identify the parameters of the problem, talk with your advisors, find out what you can do to remedy the situation, and then engage with the government. Keep in mind that sometimes these government employees love what they do, sometimes they hate what they do, but be kind. You want to be as helpful as you can on your side of the issue. Ask questions such as, "What can I do to help you?" "What do you need?" "How can I make this easier for you?" They may or may not be receptive, but you will not win any points with bureaucrats by acting out of anger (trust me, I know from firsthand experience!). Remember, they're the experts in this space. If they choose to make your life difficult, they certainly can, or they may be able to smooth the road for you. Understand that they are people doing their jobs and see how you can achieve resolution. Their job is to help you, so be grateful and don't take the bait. If they hate their life, don't take it personally.

Compliance is a necessary component of business, and most of these laws were created with good intentions. When I was a mortgage broker, I would show clients that the actual sale and loan for their home purchase consisted of three documents: the HUD, the note, and the deed. That was all that was legally needed for the transfer of ownership and to create the loan. The rest of the documents that made up the massive amount of paperwork were what I called "compliance papers that were likely a result of bureaucracy, legalese, and successful lawsuits." They were there to protect the processor, the investor, government compliance, and to cover me by making sure I followed all the necessary rules. It wasn't just for me—it was for everyone.

If you are doing your best, the likelihood of getting into real trouble is small, but it's important that you understand all the regulations for your industry. Keep any legal and financial documents or audits for the required length of time, which could be seven or more years—all the more reason to keep them together in one binder. Make sure you talk to your advisors to find out exactly what you should be doing.

I've chosen to make the government my partner. What I mean by this is that I factor in how much it will cost me—in time, treasure, and talent—to make sure I'm engaging with the government and in compliance with everything. I assume that compliance is a part of the cost of running my business. If I can't run the business and afford to pay for compliance, then I shouldn't be running the business and I need to adjust my model.

REVENUE TAKING

Another pointed reminder: *I'm not giving tax advice or legal advice.* But I'm here to let you know that the government is set to take roughly 40 percent of your net revenue (dependent on the state you live in). This is the revenue after your legitimate expenses.

In most solopreneur cases, you will likely be 100 percent personally responsible for all of the income tax that your business creates. The business entity itself typically won't pay most taxes, but the liability for those taxes will flow through to you personally. There are a variety of tools your accountant can recommend to pay fewer taxes—401(k)s, retirement plans, and other deductions. A great accountant, financial advisor, and tax planner—all working together—are immensely valuable when tax time rolls around.

Once you are generating revenue, you can and should pay yourself a salary, and that salary needs to be fair compensation for the business that you're doing. Your entity, ABC Company, pays you a salary as an employee, so you'll need to take out traditional Social Security and FICA taxes. Both the employer and employee pay this, even though you are one and the same. Let's say Medicare (1.45 percent) and FICA (6.2 percent)—for a combined total of 7.65 percent—is taken from your salary by your employer. As a manager, you will now pay both the employee and employer side for a total of over 15 percent. This is from every payroll dollar you pay yourself and before any income tax liability.

Separate from your payroll, your accountant may suggest you also pay yourself dividend payments from the company. This payment is considered a dividend on the investment you made as owner of the company and is taxed in a similar way as dividend payments you may receive on stocks you own in the stock market. In these cases, the taxes you will be obligated to pay will be different and typically much less. This is where understanding dividends, when to distribute them, and what taxes are associated with the distribution is important and why you should work with your accountant.

You might also be responsible for special taxes, depending on where you are located. In some cases, I've seen businesses be responsible for a *special tax* because they're physically located next to a stadium or in a special zone or district. Speak with your advisors in advance about these topics because the answer may affect your decision about the best location for your business. I read somewhere that California was losing up to a million people a month because of the high state taxes combined with federal taxes. It is no wonder people often complain about having the government as a partner.

I know people who moved from New Jersey to Florida because there is no personal state income tax in Florida. For these people it was as if they were receiving a massive bonus on their pensions! Each state, and some cities, have their own particular rules, regulations, legislation, or tax codes that make them more or less desirable for companies or individuals to run their business there. Be aware of the obligations that exist in your location and make your business decisions accordingly.

If your advisors don't have the necessary experience in compliance and your region's tax systems, then find someone who does. You have an obligation to get it right and know what you are signing up for! This chapter should serve to help you understand that compliance is important, and noncompliance may be the biggest killer of sound sleep and peace of mind a business owner can face.

TAKEAWAYS

- Noncompliance is one of the biggest challenges of small business.
- Draw on your entire team of advisors to determine proper government compliance.
- Budget and plan accordingly.

HOMEWORK

1. Document all your answers to the questions in this chapter to further flesh out your road map.
2. Document financial expenses from this section that will impact your start-up costs and budget.
3. Document time elements and constraints that arose out of this section.

CHAPTER THIRTEEN

BUILD YOUR SUCCESS GUIDE

———

Success is not final, failure is not fatal: it is the courage to continue that counts.

WINSTON CHURCHILL

You've interviewed the other solopreneur experts in your field, potential clients, and people in specific industries. You've found people you trust who may become your team of advisors. You've asked some difficult questions and received a wealth of answers. You've done the homework outlined in the previous chapters and filled out each page of your road map with new information and additional questions. You're now much more educated in this space! Now it's time to take a step back, reflect, and celebrate that you've come so far. You are transitioning into becoming an expert investor, manager, head of business development, salesperson, and technician. This new experience and thinking will allow you to confidently define whether this is going to be a good fit or not. You've done a lot of heavy lifting, and you are now going to formalize this by building out and refining five documents. This is a high-level introduction for what each will need to include:

- Team of Advisors: You will clearly define who they are, their area of expertise, your expectations for their help, and what they are accountable to help you with. I even include each individual's photo and bio.
- Road Map: Fully completed, step-by-step plan. This is where all your homework comes together. It is time to clean up and organize all the information you've been acquiring from your interviews and research and the conclusions you came to on the best approach for you to take.
- Financial Viability: This is where you have documented all of your *need to haves*, *should haves*, and *nice to haves*. You should list them out into different sections, starting with the *need to haves*. This will provide a good idea of how much everything will cost, at a bare minimum. From there you can confidently put on your investor hat and determine if your dream is financially viable and how much it's going to take to get started. You will define how much time and dollars it is likely to take to launch, what you need to charge, and how much you can make in the future.
- Initial Timeline to Launch: What's the right time to

start? It may be dependent on various things—seasonality, necessary financing, necessary licensure, possible contracted engagements, office space, and the other items that have been defined in your road map. Will you need certain credentials, additional education, licenses, a physical location, or specialized equipment? If any of these will take a substantial amount of time, this should be built into your timeline. If you can start your solopreneur journey as a side job and moonlight to start, great! How long do you anticipate doing this? What metrics will you track so that you will safely know when it is okay to jump ship fully into your own practice?

- Defined Accountability: Make sure you have a clear understanding of your roles as an investor, manager, head of business development, and technician. Are these roles crystal clear? Have you anticipated exactly how much time you will need and have to devote to each hat at different times during your transition? If you are going to subcontract out any aspects of your business, make sure the roles and expectations of the people you're contracting with are clear. Ensure every role is held accountable through a defined process and accountability partners.

This living guide will always be evolving and changing. However, the initial intention is to give you a rock-solid understanding and level of competence and confidence on your decision to become a solopreneur. This doesn't mean these tools are ever finished. The market and customers change, and you're constantly going to be editing, adding to, removing from, and developing these tools.

TEAM OF ADVISORS

Your advisors will be made up of four groups of people:

- Your peer network: Experts in your same industry you interviewed early on or sit on an industry board with. They may be geographically in the same area, or they may not be! These people may become your new *work* colleagues and could serve as great referral sources.
- Your potential client network: Potential and existing clients you can use as a sounding board to test your ideas, refine your product and service, and possibly become referral sources and potentially clients themselves.
- Your expert advisors: Advisors in areas of professional expertise that you will be using, namely an accountant, attorney, insurance expert, and banker. These are experts you turn to when you need answers or advice.
- Your accountability partner or accountability network: This is the group that will help hold your feet to the fire to make sure you're following through with what you need to do. If you are struggling and looking

for professional advice or facilitation, you can join a virtual pro circle at aspiringsolopreneur.com.

These people will be ones you can trust, and they will be invaluable throughout the life of your solopreneur journey. Build and maintain these relationships. They can introduce you to other experts and potential clients. They can be a great resource for you, and you can be a great resource for them. They will help you avoid most of the missteps and empower you to thrive and live your best life.

ROAD MAP

The road map is a culmination of all the questions, answers, and research you've gathered throughout this book. Included will be the analysis of your competitive environment, your ideal client, and your unique value proposition. You will also have all the completed interviews.

The road map helps you to get a clearer understanding of your journey ahead. It empowers you by making sure you have the available tools and are very clear about your plan. A documents binder is a great centralized place to hold all these findings.

FINANCIAL VIABILITY

The Financial Viability (often referred to as your "pro forma") is a financial assessment used to project your income and monthly costs to calculate profit. It is a key step to determining if your success guide is viable. You will be incorporating all the answers on finances that you've gathered in your interviews and any research you've conducted.

The Financial Viability can be overwhelming, so take it step by step. It's critical to gather this information before you start. Knowing this information will help you sleep at night! In this section I will be helping you to outline expenses, calculate the necessary earnings to cover those expenses, compare those numbers, and calculate the burn rate to see how much money you need to launch. Don't worry, it won't be painful.

CALCULATING EXPENSES

There are three types of expenses: start-up, fixed monthly costs, and variable costs. List them all out on separate pages.

- Begin with your start-up costs. This could be education, licenses, setting up your business entity, a website, preliminary marketing, first/last month's rent, and so on. This encompasses all your *need to haves* that you will spend money on once to get up and running.

- Next, calculate your fixed monthly costs. These are the costs of keeping the doors open each month and can include rent, software subscriptions, base inventory, insurance, equipment leasing, and so on. For example, if you're an attorney, you need an office, a phone, insurance, leases on equipment, accounting, bookkeeping, and possibly a virtual assistant. These expenses will typically be monthly, regardless of whether you bring in revenue or not.
- Next calculate the variable costs. These are items that fluctuate depending on the number of people you engage with each month. This could be raw materials, packaging, and any tasks you plan to outsource. In some cases, variable costs may be minimal, but in others they may be substantial.

Once you have these expenses outlined, you can begin to get a better understanding of the necessary costs to start and run the business. You can then determine how many clients you will need to at least cover your monthly costs.

CALCULATING EARNINGS TO COVER EXPENSES

Many people try to figure out how much they need to earn hourly by doing the following: Take monthly costs, divide by four weeks per month, and forty hours per week.

If their expenses are $8,000, they determine they must earn $50 each hour to cover expenses.

Unfortunately, that's not accurate, and this type of thinking is exclusively that of a technician. You first need to assess how many hours you have available each month to work as a technician. Some of your hours may be spent as the investor, manager, or in business development. All of these are important, but none of these are billable hours. The likelihood of having forty hours of billable time each week isn't reasonable at the start. In fact, when you are starting out, you will likely spend much more time in areas that don't result in billable hours but are still absolutely necessary. Your billable hours may only be twenty hours a week or less when you start. You'll have to figure that out for yourself.

Using the example, if your monthly expenses are $8,000 and you have a handful of initial clients in place so you know you can bill for twenty-five hours a week as a technician, you actually need to bill at $80 an hour just to cover the costs. Keep in mind, this is before you're recouping your start-up costs and earning an income. This is where your investor and manager hats may need to review your *need to haves* and *should haves* again.

Note: This is for typical monthly operating expenses. Any additional revenue will help you determine how quickly

you can pay off your initial start-up costs and begin to get
a return on that investment as the business owner/investor.

MAKE A COMPARISON

Now take a step back and assess your current employed situation. Take your current salary and add 7.65 percent of that number to back in FICA and Medicare—remembering that your employer is already matching that. Add in any car allowance or extra benefits. Add in healthcare, insurance, worker's compensation, and other benefits. How much is this new number? Many in the entrepreneurial world refer to this as the "fully loaded employee cost," and it's usually around 130 to 180 percent of what someone actually receives in compensation pre-tax. As an example, let's say you're an attorney and your gross salary at the firm where you work as an employee is $100,000. When you factor in all the extras and benefits, it would not be out of line to say your fully loaded cost to the firm is upwards of $150,000. This is your starting financial reference point and gives you an idea of where you are *currently* compared to where you *want to go.*

Just remember: breathe! Try not to get overwhelmed. This is exciting! You are empowering yourself with the tools to go into your decision with your eyes wide open!

CALCULATE THE BURN RATE

The burn rate is a basic way of determining whether you have enough runway to launch your business or if you are going to run out of runway before liftoff.

That runway is literally the dollars you will need to have set aside to launch your business after you have deducted your start-up costs. Take this number and divide by the monthly expenses projected. This number shows you how many months you can go without a paycheck before burning through your launch savings and having to go look for a job.

Look at your personal monthly budget and assess approximately how long it will take until you start bringing in income from your new solopreneur life. If you have $6,500 in monthly expenses and project it will take ten months to start bringing a profit to your business, you'll want at least an additional $65,000 in the bank to cover your living expenses. This will be a factor in your burn rate as well. Once you have these numbers, you will need to be comfortable with the time frame you anticipate it will take to launch. With time frames, I always suggest multiplying your anticipated months by 1.5 because start-up always takes longer than anticipated.

If you end up not needing the money you projected, great! You're that much further ahead. You can make this model even more sophisticated by starting to factor in certain revenue steps and increases as you go—in other words, if you can project estimated income each month when you are certain it will come in. If you know you have a contract starting in three months at $5,000 a month, this income can be used to offset some of the expenses. I suggest being conservative as you build these steps in, but they will increase your runway. This will decrease the overall capital needed to launch.

Most people should budget for a six- to twelve-month burn rate minimum. I personally budgeted $100,000 for my first year of transitioning to my latest solopreneur life with Entrepreneurial Advisors. This was right after I sold a company and was transitioning 100 percent into advisory work. The money was spent on training, certifications, and marketing, along with business expenses. None of this was invested in paying any of my personal bills. During this time, I did not take a salary. My wife was working, and we had good savings; however, it took close to a year before the scales tipped to where I covered all the expenses, recouped my start-up costs, and replaced the income I had previously been earning. In the grand scheme of things, this was pretty quick, but before I even sold the previous company, I was already doing advisory work. I had a foot in that world and knew where I was going. It wasn't a matter of *if* I would be successful, but a matter of *when* I would be successful. I had an ultralong runway—literally years if I needed it—if things didn't go the way I had hoped. My choice to launch was a no-brainer and transition into this new life. Today our finances couldn't be stronger, and I couldn't imagine living any other lifestyle.

If the monthly burn rate looks too high or your runway is too long, this is the time to explore ways to lower the monthly expenses or increase the length of time you have to achieve your goals—or perhaps a variation of both. Review your *need to haves*, *should haves*, and *nice to haves*. Perhaps you can make minor adjustments to your lifestyle or your partner can contribute more to the income. Maybe there's a way to be smarter about your transition. I am a huge fan of slow transitions and moonlighting, but sometimes that can be a challenge if you're in an organization where you have signed a noncompete agreement. Some noncompete clauses extend after you leave a company as well. If you have a noncompete, definitely discuss this with your legal counsel. You can figure it out.

The burn rate is a necessary calculation because it helps you assess finances before you jump ship and leave your current job. By preparing well now, your transition results in a minimal impact in the future. In some cases, your current employer may be okay with your transition; they may even contract with you for the portion of the work you currently handle. The ideal situation is to have a handful of contracts ready before you leave so that you're already working before you fully launch your full solopreneur life. The reason for having these early customers is to appease the investor in you. Those contracts ensure you are at least covering your expenses. Perhaps you're not making as much as you'd like, but you are now decreasing your burn rate dramatically and transitioning into your own, self-directed life.

These calculations should offer you a strong assessment of whether it's time to move ahead. Your calculations may clearly say *full steam ahead*, or you may see that it's a little tight. You'll need to be completely candid with yourself and ask yourself as the investor if this is the best idea. You very well may end up saying that you have no idea how your current employer can afford to pay you what they do, and you are so glad you don't have to worry about any of these extraneous details! Congratulations! As a leadership advisor, it never ceases to amaze me to see that people are being paid more than they would if they went on their own. Sometimes, if you're at a larger firm, you may be getting comped over and above what you could make as a solopreneur. You may realize that some of those people at the top are not making nearly the amount of money you expected, even though they have the appearance of it. As a solopreneur, you're going to have to be the investor who manages the investment and your books, so you have to make that call. You have to sit down, weigh the pros and cons, and make a decision.

Perhaps you discover you want to stay with your company or consider moving to another firm that has a better fit with your True North. This is a victory! It doesn't mean you can't go back to the drawing board for a solopreneur life—you can. You can reinvent and find a niche that is a better fit. Start trying to figure out where you can, and do, fit. This is rarely a linear process.

Or maybe all the numbers look great and you're ready to move forward. You may think, "This is a no-brainer! I've got to do this!"

Right on. Go get it!

TIMELINE

The purpose of a timeline is to figure out all the necessary steps before opening your doors and getting paid for your product or service. You may need to borrow space, pay for advertising, obtain licensure, draft contracts, or create a business structure. This requires planning and establishing benchmarks.

Go through each page of your road map and do the following:

- Identify each task necessary to launch
- Identify the length of time needed to complete the task
- Identify if the task requires a previous task to be completed first
- Identify if there is a specific time that the task must be started

Launching your solopreneur life may have some complex timelines. For example, you will be required to file a tax return and pay taxes for your company for the year in which you register it. Will you have clients during that year? If it's currently November, you may want to wait to set up the company structure in January if you expect your first clients then. This will allow you to avoid paying the extra accounting expense to file taxes for a two-month year. Make sure you're always thinking and calculating ahead. This process allows you to reverse engineer the things that will have to happen for your successful launch.

If you know that it will take six months to build enough content and a following on social media to land your first client, start in advance as part of your timeline before leaving your current position. Complete as many of the preparatory tasks as you can before leaving your job.

Return to the timeline and make sure that you understand where you currently stand, while always keeping in mind that you should be preparing and talking to people to attract those first clients.

PLAN A SMOOTH TRANSITION

As you consider your timeline and your burn rate, you may decide that you need a transition period to shift slowly into your solopreneur life without quitting your salaried job. I am a huge fan of this approach if at all possible. This path allows you to slowly build your client base on the nights and weekends while giving you the opportunity to refine what you're doing and gaining confidence in your newfound roles. You want to ultimately take the guesswork out of success so you can move further down the learning curve quicker and with less, or no, risk.

Take time to review your initial motivations back in chapter one. Don't lose sight of what you're trying to do in the first place. The challenge is, now that you're fully accountable for everything, you may have just traded one hamster wheel for another.

As you work through this transition period and start to take on clients, things will eventually build. You'll get to the point where your side gig is all consuming and you potentially have your basic monthly expenses covered and possibly pay yourself a small salary. You may not necessarily be making huge money yet, but you will be so much further down the learning curve that you'll be able to safely and smoothly consider giving notice at your existing job and transitioning into your solopreneur life. This is the ideal structure that people should shoot for.

Make sure you've done all of your research, and your financial viability and burn rate will provide an idea of how long it will take to begin earning a profit. For your proposed launch day you may pick a point and back into it. For example, through your research you might learn of a big trade show in four months. Prepare for it as you remain in your current position, and then give your notice a few weeks before the trade show. It helps to think like a chess player: plan several moves ahead, and move multiple pieces at a time to win the game. Moving a single piece at a time is typically an inefficient use of your time.

At the end of this exercise, you will have established a timeline with fixed, defined steps so that you can then make the call on what you're going to do and when.

DEFINED ACCOUNTABILITY

Accountability is very important for each of the roles you'll now be fulfilling. In this particular case, setting expectations for these roles sounds a bit like a split-personality exercise, but it's very important to define those simple three to five things that you have to be 100 percent accountable for in each role you will be occupying as the investor, manager, head of business development, and technician. Examples include:

- The investor should ensure that the investment is safe, that the business is following through on the plan as written, and that money is not being spent frivolously. That role has to make sure that, with the resources available, the focus is on the *need to haves* and driving to profitability.
- The manager should make sure you are deploying your assets, time, treasure, and talent in the right ways. They also need to do accounting, scheduling, manage the business, and ensure the head of business development and technician are investing the necessary time and staying focused.
- The head of business development is focused on introducing the business to the right people, connecting, and driving new sales. I can't stress enough how important this role is during the launch phase.
- The technician is obligated to execute the project or task in a timely fashion, to the highest quality and standards, on time and on budget.

Each role has multiple responsibilities and is key to the overarching success of the organization. That's the intention in defining the high-level accountabilities for each role, even though they are all you. You need to know what you are accountable for and what success in each role looks like.

PUTTING IT ALL TOGETHER

You have your advisory list, your road map, your financial viability, your timeline, and your defined accountabilities. Invest the time to clean up the documents and organize them into something you are proud of. Use proper headers, a basic logo, and quality paper. Print ten copies and number each on the cover page.

And then congratulate yourself because, when combined together, you have created an amazing business plan! This becomes a presentation you can hand to a potential advisor for feedback. You can show it to your partner/spouse and say, "This is all the research I've conducted and my projections for moving forward." You can potentially take it to an advisor, banker, or investor, and say, "At this point I don't need funds, but here is the goal, and I might need a loan at a later point." When you hand out the documents, people will understand the value and time you've invested. This type of groundwork sets you far above anyone else and truly sets you up for success.

You've gone through the entire process of creating a great business plan, perhaps without even realizing it!

I've done this hundreds of times and, candidly, rarely do I actually finish a business plan before I realize the business is something I don't want to do, wouldn't be great at, or shouldn't do. I consider these huge victories.

It should be the same for you. If, after you have reviewed your plan, you need to pivot or make adjustments, that's a success. Look at how much smarter you are now.

At aspiringsolopreneur.com, this process is available with tools and self-paced video instruction for a Solopreneur Certification. This is also the exact process I go through in the live, virtual, and professionally facilitated Solopreneur Success Camps. They are held online and include these exercises, group facilitation, additional tools, and accountability.

TAKEAWAYS

- All of the work you've done so far should be enough information to confidently decide if being a solopreneur is a good fit for you.
- Financial viability has allowed you to calculate the expenses and your burn rate.
- A complete timeline has allowed you to determine launch steps and a launch date.
- It is crucial to be clear on what every role is accountable for.

HOMEWORK

1. Build out five foundational documents of the success guide: Team of Advisors, Road Map, Financial Viability, Initial Timeline to Launch, and Defined Accountabilities.

2. Work through your financial viability and determine estimated expenses and burn rate.

3. Build your transition timeline and the steps to launch your thriving solopreneur life.

4. Gather any handwritten notes and type them out. Add logos, branding, contracts, and agreements, and organize everything into your success guide binder. You now have a business plan and success guide!

CHAPTER FOURTEEN

REVIEW YOUR BUSINESS PLAN & ASK YOURSELF THE TOUGH QUESTIONS

———

We only do no-brainers.

CHARLIE MUNGER

You've created a fully built, kickass business plan. You've done the hard interviews and now you're going to be looking at starting your solopreneur journey with the sophistication of a potential client, an investor, manager, head of business development, and technician.

Through this process you have gained a clear understanding of what it will take to be successful and can look at the plan from the different roles. This doesn't mean you can necessarily answer every remaining question or solve every problem, but you do know who to ask or where to research further, answer, and minimize the risk associated with them. You're starting to become an expert in understanding all the components needed for success.

Go through your business plan—it should be mostly filled out by now, with only a few questions left to ask. You may be able to fill in those holes yourself now that you've gone through this experience. If you can't, this is where you go back and meet with your advisors again. Or do additional research. Do whatever it takes to answer those questions. You are so much more sophisticated than when you first opened this book, and now you know which questions to ask.

You may have received conflicting advice from your advisors, and now it's time to dig in and choose. Decide who should make this decision. Is it you as the investor? You as the manager? You as the head of business development? Or you as the technician? There may even be an internal struggle as you decide who gets to answer!

This is also the time to address whether the solopreneur path is one you really want, and are you still aligned with your partner/spouse? Your significant other needs to fully understand the road ahead, and sharing the business plan will showcase the time and effort you've put into your research. It will help them alleviate or minimize any fears, and hopefully they will champion your "no-brainer" of an idea. You approached them at the beginning of the journey with your idea, but now you know exactly what it will take. Will they be your greatest source of encouragement and support?

I have found in most cases if there is a relationship conflict around a business start-up, it is typically a result of a partner being surprised and scared when bad news is sprung on them. In these cases, they often act more reactionary. The tolerance level of a partner is typically much higher when someone is proactive and planning. Your partner needs to be in total alignment for this to be a success. I've seen people hide bad things from their spouse and they don't find out until the car is repossessed or the credit cards have a $50,000 balance with nothing to show for it. This won't be you! Make sure to show your partner all your homework. Get them on board and act as a team! Be open and honest and communicate with one another. Make sure everybody's eyes are wide open! Ideally all while still employed as a technician in your current job. I promise you, when you are both in alignment, it can be spectacular!

LIFE ANALYSIS

You have an idea about what the future commitment looks like and how much time and money it will take to launch your solopreneur life. You've gone from theoretical to practical. Now it's time to address if it's going to be a good life fit.

Look at every element, including time, dollars, and especially personal accountability. You may need to spend 50 percent of your time doing business development and another 20 percent building the business and getting things ready before you even start actually doing billable work. That time is going to cost you money, and it may take six to twelve months before you're actually up and running. Do you have enough funds in the bank? How long is your burn rate? Is your partner aligned with your decision? Is this within your comfort zone?

Once you start, it may take eighty-hour weeks for the first three to twelve months to get the business launched. You may be working for free or less money than you currently bring in at your place of employment. Do you feel that this is the best, highest use of your time? Are you leveraging your talents in the way that you really want to? What sort of treasure will it take to get where you want to be? Will the future returns be worth the investment today? If you have made it this far, I'm guessing it will be.

Be candid with yourself. If you know you are not a self-starter, you'll need an accountability partner. Or perhaps you've determined it will take a $100,000 runway to be comfortable for you to step away from your current position, and you only have $30,000 in the bank. Decide how or where you can save another $70,000 before you pull the trigger. This can be frustrating, but being frustrated is better than going bankrupt. Own that! It's better to get frustrated and figure these things out now and make an educated decision. If you need any further advice, consider joining the Solopreneur Success Camp or One-on-One Advisory Coaching at aspiringsolopreneur.com.

Look at the positives and the negatives. It doesn't have to be difficult to become a solopreneur and make this transition. Now that you have a better idea of what it's really going to take to be a solopreneur, will your motivations be fulfilled? Will you be able to spend those afternoons with your kids and go to every soccer game? Can you make more money? Will you be the master of your own time? Can you be accountable for self-starting, for accountability, and for making sure everything gets paid? Make sure that you feel comfortable with everything. The journey is worth it!

BUSINESS ANALYSIS

Look at the business and the business plan you've built and ask yourself if starting this business is a no-brainer from the point of view of four different roles.

- The investor. If your friend or family member handed

you your exact business plan and financial viability and asked for $100,000, would you, if you had it to give, feel comfortable offering the money based on his experience and effort? Is it safe? What return will you see on your investment? Is the risk worth it? Is this a no-brainer?

- The manager. Is this something that is easy to manage, you're able to do it, and you would find it fun? What is the market rate for this role, and can you afford to pay yourself in this capacity? Is this a no-brainer?

- The head of business development. Seeing this business plan and knowing yourself, would you hire yourself to go out and bring in the volume of business you will need to be successful? Will you be successful at it? Is this a no-brainer?

- The technician. Would you want to work for a business that looks like this? What should this position pay as an employee-technician? If you look at that dollar figure, would this be a company and job you'd want to work for at that rate? Is it a good fit? And will you ultimately enjoy all of this and will it fulfill your True North and motivations? Is this a no-brainer?

Does this whole process sound like it will be fun? Are you enthused about acting as an investor, manager, head of business development, and a technician? Life's too short. Embrace the life you can have.

THE PATH FORWARD

What does it look like when the choice is clearly to move forward with a solopreneur launch?

I once worked with an attorney who was employed at a large corporate firm where he charged his clients $400 per hour. Unfortunately, as with most large firms, the firm had a lot of expenses he had to contribute to, including travel, fancy offices, business development, sports tickets, sponsors, advertising, and marketing. The partners also received a share of his earnings, so he made far less than he charged. He decided to explore going out on his own.

He ran the numbers, did the analysis, spoke to advisors, gathered insurance quotes, looked at spaces, and assessed his financial viability. As part of his motivations he realized he loved patent law. He could do a great job being a small patent attorney and charge $300 per hour. It would allow him to transition into his own private practice with one office, and he could handle the work himself. He would be able to work thirty fewer hours a month but actually increase his income and have the flexibility to spend more time with his family, which was important to him. He had no noncompete and great relationships with people in the community. It was a no-brainer for him.

If you do the research and assessments and realize that it's kind of close, but it's not quite there, then it's not a no-brainer. And if it's not a no-brainer, then I suggest that you stop and assess what adjustments it would take to make it a no-brainer.

LET GO OF THE FANTASY

Some people may desperately want to work for themselves, but their first idea doesn't pan out. They may have a hard time letting go of this first idea and feel deflated because they've invested time and energy on something that they were excited about. I would urge people to reframe that thinking. Through this book you've been on a journey to educate yourself. You are much more informed and when you choose to pull the trigger, and it is a no-brainer, you will be much more successful.

Some people fall in love with the idea of something in their head, but they're not willing to see the reality of that idea's implication. They don't assess properly and instead charge full steam ahead. They think, "This is my one shot. I'm never going to be able to do this again." PLEASE stop and know that's not true. I've actually gone through this entire exercise and journey hundreds of times. Most of the time when I stopped and took a very hard look at the research, I came to the conclusion that it wasn't a no-brainer. This is where you have to be protective of your time, of your investments, and really work toward your skillset. Review what you have, tweak it, adjust it, pivot, and if it looks like a win, dig back in.

It doesn't mean that working for yourself as a solopreneur is completely off the table. Far from it. What it means is that the current direction that you looked at may not make sense. If you're trying desperately to get this plan to succeed because you hate your job, or you hate your manager, and you dread getting out of bed, it's time to take a deep breath. Know that you have turned on some switches in your head that will expand your way of thinking. You will now start seeing opportunities everywhere. The more you cultivate and explore these opportunities, the more you're going to grow and see what's possible. As you move ahead, you'll start to have other business ideas or opportunities that appear on your radar.

When you choose to not try and force a round peg into a square hole, that's where you're going to find success. Take the time to figure out the right niche that is your ideal fit and you know you can excel in, instead of forcing yourself into a niche where you're unhappy or failing and going back into the same doom loop you currently work in. It may take you six months, a year, or even five years to find that niche, but it's better to do that than to hope a poor fit will work. You may find a niche but need to hone your skillset before moving forward. Perhaps you need more education or a different direction. Will your current employer help pay for education? If so, that's perfect. You get double the value for your time. You're getting a paycheck, you're contributing to your workplace, and you're also sharpening the tools necessary for transition and building a plan to a solopreneur life at the same time.

When you know in your heart it's a no-brainer, you know it! Dive in and go for it.

TAKEAWAYS

- Your kick-ass business plan is fully built out.
- It is important to analyze your life and business to determine if this is a no-brainer.
- This is not your "one shot"—you can go on this journey multiple times.

HOMEWORK

1. Review your business plan.
2. Conduct a life and business analysis.
3. Do a final assessment and determine if this solopreneur venture is a no-brainer.

PART FOUR

LIVE YOUR DREAM LIFE

CHAPTER FIFTEEN

EXECUTE TIMELINE FOR A SMOOTH TRANSITION

———

You are never too old to set a new goal or dream a new dream.

C. S. LEWIS

Everything you've done up to this point has been an evolution in your thinking and education through interviews, research, self-assessment, and decision-making. Now it's time to make the call, pull the trigger, and execute. There are a lot of mechanics to be considered. Establish your business entity, identify key clients, get new contracts, identify a location, resource any material requirements, and consider your financials. You've got this.

ESSENTIAL FEATURES IN EXECUTION

As I have discussed, when it comes to organization and

execution, you'll need to assess what business features are *need to haves*, *should haves*, and *nice to haves* to start. Keep it simple on all fronts. Invest in first things first: this means looking at your timeline and road map and investing time and money in accordance to your plan.

- Think about the items a client absolutely needs to see when they look at you and your operation. Start with the bare minimum, not the premium showroom or penthouse office. Remember: at this point, being done is often better than perfect.
- Return to your business plan and determine how you are going to do business development and begin to attract clients. If you want to be a "thought leader," a website and/or blog may be a great place to start. I'm currently advising a solopreneur in the UK who is an expert in climate change and the global sciences. He's currently an academic and a professor, but he is not happy with where he is in life and wants to transition into owning his own business. He decided he needed a minimum of a year to focus on building thought leadership via writing blog content and white papers, attending speaking events, and social networking. This will be beneficial to the university he works for as well as for him personally, but he's making sure to build his own personal brand with the intention of getting hired for consulting gigs on the side, to start, and potentially full time in the future.

Think of ways you can build yourself as a thought leader as well.

- Set up a structure for your organization that you and your advisors have concluded will be best. Listen to what they suggest, identify the right timing, and get it done.
- Establish a plan for basic bookkeeping. If you only have a handful of accounts or transactions, you can begin on a yellow pad or an Excel spreadsheet. Simplicity and consistency are key. Make sure you stay current. Getting behind can turn into a mess. I speak from experience here.
- List out and schedule the networking functions you will need to attend, and make them a priority. Make the manager role push the head of business development to get out there. Remember, it's more important to attend the right networking functions where you will get in front of the right potential clients.
- Define where you will be working: from an office, the basement, or a shared space. It doesn't necessarily need to be fancy, but it does need to be defined.
- Establish the work hours for your new gig. Even while still employed, schedule the hours you are at your "second job" getting things organized. This could mean you schedule three nights a week from 7:00 to 9:00 p.m. and four hours on Saturday. Make the manager enforce the hours. You want to make that investor happy, and it is a great habit to cultivate.

With your investor hat on, encourage yourself as the manager, head of business development, and technician. Do you, as technician, need to invest time on a logo and website? Put on your investor hat and tell yourself it's unnecessary. Do you, as manager, want to rent an expensive suite? Put on your investor hat and tell yourself that you only require a shared office space. It's helpful to develop this split personality with yourself. And when you make these bigger decisions, bring your accountability partner or advisor on board or ask yourself, "As an investor, would I make this investment? As a manager, is this the right thing for business?" Have these internal debates and hold yourself accountable.

I knew a group of people who started a software company. They had watched too many start-up shows with investors on TV and knew the words "A round funding" and "B round funding." They had heard the word "traunch" and decided they needed to have the most designer office space imaginable. All of these words are related to the venture capital and angel investor space—which I believe can be a giant distraction to most start-ups. They became distracted finding and answering to the money instead of building and driving their business.

So they leased a corner office and filled it with a foosball table, beer in the fridge, an open plan, and skateboards *instead* of realizing that what they actually needed was great software and clients who were purchasing it. It wasn't that they didn't deserve it, but this group wasted untold time, treasure, and talent thinking about their image as a hip start-up in a fancy office instead of building a company that could be known for its stellar software. In this particular case it was a start-up business, but the same principles can apply to solopreneurs. Lean on your split personality—the investor, the manager, the head of business development, and technician—and decide if this is the best thing you need at this point in time.

CLIENTS ARE THE KEY TO SUCCESS

The 1989 movie *Field of Dreams* has the fabulous tagline of "If you build it, they will come." It's a wonderful premise for a movie, but it's a terrible premise for starting a business. The key when you're starting as a solopreneur is to figure out what you need to do to generate revenue.

For a new venture to be successful, what is the one thing you absolutely, positively need? Clients. It may sound corny, but when people first transition, the thing many solopreneurs are most afraid of is finding clients. You can have the nicest office in the city, you can be the greatest expert in your field, you can have bookkeeping and compliance in effect; but if you don't have clients, it means nothing.

Most people resist business development activities

because they are afraid they will be rejected. You might get rejected, and you might get knocked down. But the manager and investor in you will need to positively encourage the business developer in you to get back out there, head down, and keep swinging. You can have the greatest business plan in the world, but until you actually trip and fall, pick yourself up, dust yourself off, and keep going, you're not really prepared for success or for what's to come.

Perhaps everything goes great, exactly according to plan. If so, wonderful, but that's highly unusual. Steal Silicon Valley's idea to "fail fast." Once you have your first client, do the best you can. If you fall down or screw up—and you will sometimes—do what's necessary to quickly save that relationship. Be prepared to make mistakes. Figure out where you failed, figure out exactly what your client needs, and then iterate to make your product or service a little better. And then iterate again and iterate again and iterate again...and you will eventually not only find success, but begin to thrive.

Please note, I'm not talking anyone into creating challenges! Remember that every time you fail, change the narrative in your head and embrace how you're finding a way to improve and you're moving up the learning curve toward success.

You may have to make adjustments. Get your offering 80 percent of the way there and start presenting to potential clients. Get them to help you define the last 20 percent. This will empower you to create something they really want and is likely a little different than you would have originally done it. Those who wait six months to get things absolutely perfect before finally opening their doors often find that people no longer want their particular services or products in the way they are presenting it, or they want a different version. Everything has to be changed, which may take another few months. If, instead, they started at 80 percent with clients, they could adjust and fail and adjust again along the way.

WHEN TO JUMP SHIP?

You should not jump ship from your day job until you've answered any outstanding questions, and your choice to launch your solopreneur life has become a no-brainer.

- ☐ You are clear on your True North and motivations.
- ☐ You have an expert board of advisors you trust and have put together your advisory list.
- ☐ You have a completed, refined, and documented road map.
- ☐ You have completed, refined, and documented your idea's financial viability and know your burn rate and how long your runway will last.

- [ ] You have a completed, refined, and documented timeline.
- [ ] You have defined accountability for all your hats and advisors.
- [ ] You have reviewed all of your research with your partner and have their full support.
- [ ] You have clients not only identified, but committed and ready to go forward.
- [ ] You know what it will cost and have funds available for transition.
- [ ] You have clearly defined and abided by your *need to have*, *should have*, and *nice to have* list.
- [ ] You have a support/accountability group/person scheduled for weekly check-ins to assure accountability.
- [ ] You know the business structure you will go with and who will create it for you.
- [ ] You have a clear plan for bookkeeping and compliance and the person who will help with that identified.
- [ ] You have listed out your key networking groups and scheduled out where and when you will be attending.
- [ ] You may be on an industry board or two.
- [ ] You know where you will work.
- [ ] You have scheduled your work hours for the first ninety days.
- [ ] You have time blocked out and scheduled for business development.
- [ ] Wearing your investor hat, you would be willing to invest in your business.

- ☐ Wearing your manager hat, you are excited to build and manage yourself and this business.
- ☐ Wearing your head of business development hat, you have clients in place, and you are excited about building a pipeline of more business.
- ☐ Wearing your technician hat, you've become an expert in your niche and have all the necessary certifications and qualifications and can't wait to get started.
- ☐ Pulling the trigger now is a NO-BRAINER.

Congratulations! You have completed a monumental shift in your thinking. You are ready.

When you are finally prepared to execute, you will be leaving your employer, company, and colleagues behind and embracing your dream. I am a huge believer in karma and that what goes around comes around. I recommend that when you leave, that you do so on the highest ethical terms possible. Remember, this is your first true act as a new business owner. Treat others how you want to be treated. I can't tell you how many new solopreneurs get referrals from their previous employer. How you leave your current job matters!

Give proper adequate notice and be as gracious and grateful as you can possibly be. However, be fully prepared to receive pushback and potential nastiness from people. This reaction isn't necessarily about you personally as much as it reflects the insecurities of others. People may react negatively because you're doing something they lack the courage to do. You may hear, "Oh, that's stupid. You're going to fail." Understand that you're hearing their insecurities talking. This isn't your reality. You have done the research and know what you're in for. Resist the urge to react, and don't burn any bridges as you leave. Your former colleagues, clients, or associates could become your best clients, so *always* take the high ground.

Once you've formally jumped ship, you've begun your journey. Congratulations! The momentum will hopefully start rolling, and you now need to build the discipline to wear all four hats: the investor needs to hold the manager accountable for running the business, the head of business development needs to make sure to drive the business, and the technician needs to execute the business.

TAKEAWAYS

- Determine the essential features for execution.
- Test and refine.
- Review the final checklist.
- Make the call on when you will step into your new life

HOMEWORK

1. Complete the checklist to determine when to fully jump ship from your day job.

2. Determine your *need to haves*, *should haves*, and *nice to haves*.

3. Establish logistics: work hours, bookkeeping, organization, and workspace.

CHAPTER SIXTEEN

NAVIGATE THE FIRST SIX MONTHS LIKE A PRO

———

If you want to get somewhere you have to know where you want to go and how to get there. Then never, never, never give up.

NORMAN VINCENT PEALE

The first six months of your solopreneur life may be completely different from anything you've done before. This period can be like a new relationship in that it's fun and exciting, but at the same time it can be frustrating and a bit like playing whack-a-mole or living the movie *Groundhog Day* because you may need to wake up and do the same thing over and over.

Realize that if you make mistakes, it is okay. Everybody does. Mistakes are wonderful. What makes the difference is how you learn from them, what you learn from them, and how you can be humbled and grateful for them. You've done your research; you know the steps you need to take for success. Work your plan and get busy. It's time to get clients!

BE ACCOUNTABLE

Getting new clients may be hard work if you don't have a contract or clients right from the start. Remember, you can't just turn on the lights and expect that people will show up. However, if you've done all the preliminary work, you have plans in place and only need to remain accountable to see your plans through. You need to remain accountable to yourself. Determine what needs to be done to drive sales and how many business development appointments you need to make—whether it be on the phone or face-to-face. The manager needs to hold the head of business development accountable: it's time to work on prospecting and bringing in new clients, get on the phone, and have face-to-face meetings. Get out to the network meetings in your industry. Drop off information and marketing materials to the people in your niche. Update your social media platforms consistently. Accomplish your first-things-first goals and be accountable to your manager self.

Accountability is key at this point of the journey. You

have to make sure that you wear your manager hat so you don't slack off. Set and schedule your work hours and get dressed to go to work—even if your office is downstairs. The first time you put on your suit and walk to the basement drinking a cup of coffee, you may think, "Huh, well, what am I supposed to do?" And this is where you split your personality, prepare your four hats, and say out loud, "Okay, I'm the manager here, and there are some things that need to get done. And as the head of business development, I need A, B, and C done today." With your hats on, manage your time and make sure the other roles follow through.

If you want to give yourself a thirty-minute break for lunch, that's fine. If you decide to take two hours in the middle of the day to watch your daughter's soccer game, great; but you, as the manager, may require that the technician or head of business development works late that night for two extra hours. In some cases, you may work a lot more than you currently are to start. In other cases you'll work less, but if you don't establish good habits, you'll slide into bad ones. Time block as needed. Bad habits allow you to be distracted by the laundry, light bulbs, Candy Crush, Facebook, and other diversions. Zealously watch out for these time hijacks.

PRO TIP: TIME BLOCK

There are very convincing studies that suggest that our social platforms and handheld devices are not saving us time; rather, they are actually giant distractions that lead to inefficiency. It's documented that in transitioning between hearing the ping of an email, reading the email, responding to the email, and getting back to focus on their original task, people lose three times the time the actual task took. This is a hijack of their cognitive ability. This is incredibly inefficient. If you can stay focused on one task for a fixed period of time, you give yourself a substantial bonus in time. Consider thirty- to sixty-minute focused blocks.

Remember, all of your smart phones and other devices have airplane mode or the ability to be turned off. If you think people are going to call you, turn everything off but the ringing of the phone. If you decide to make calls, do nothing but make calls for one or two hours. Block out your time and then stay focused on only the task at hand.

If you decide to spend time on your logo, fine. Give yourself a set period of time, say thirty minutes. But outside of that, you need to focus on other things. It's really easy to let everything slip, and the more you can focus on one thing at a time, the more efficiently you will accomplish your goals. Multitasking is a myth—it doesn't work. If you time block the activity, you increase the likelihood of getting it done.

WHAT HAPPENS WHEN YOU SLIP?

For most people, it's not a matter of if you will slip, it's just a matter of when! Everybody does, but how you address the slip will have a big impact. If you do slip, make sure to forgive yourself, but then hold yourself accountable for the future. Make sure it doesn't become a habit.

As an example, I have a successful client who is a financial planner, and I helped him transition from working with a large financial planning firm to his own private practice. He did all of the legwork to get where he needed to. Before launch, he had to jump through a lot of hoops in regard to his noncompete and compliance. He legally wasn't allowed to have preliminary conversations with clients before he left the company. When he finally got ready to transition to his own practice, it was a huge achievement.

He is brilliant and hardworking; however, his challenge was that he talked himself into believing he wasn't the biggest fan of business development. He was free to call his clients now, but he really didn't like "sales" calls. Instead of spending the first thirty days as a solopreneur calling as many clients as possible, he let himself get distracted with business mechanics. He spent time on the logo and the perfect promotional pieces instead of talking to dozens of clients a day to capture as many of the people who loved working with him as possible. This critical piece wasn't fun for him, so he mostly avoided it or, at a minimum, did not do as much as he could have done.

PRO TIP: CREATE A GOAL BOARD

In some cases, people will build a goal board or dream board. This may have two sections. One is the dream side. This has visualizations as well as specific action items of things they need to do. It could involve pictures of your children, vacation ideas, and items you want to purchase. I have seen these include a fancy new house, the Eiffel Tower representing a trip to France, a private plane, and symbols of college for kids. I believe there is something magical that happens when you do this sort of visualization.

The second side would be more activity and metrics based. What are the specific activities you will need to do on a weekly basis to achieve these dreams? These may be sales or performance based.

This can be a board or big piece of foam core placed someplace you will see it daily. It's typically private and something that you can hang on the back of your door and will serve to remind you of what you're doing, why you're doing it, and how you're going to get there.

We had a conversation eighteen months into his solopreneur business, and I asked, "What was the one thing you would've done differently?" He replied that he would have been more disciplined about making business development client calls in the first three months as it would have made considerable difference with his current business. His estimations were that his book of business could have been 30 percent larger (or more) if he would have only focused on making calls in those three months instead of focusing on the logo, and so on.

The reality is, most of us don't like the idea of some business development tasks. We build it up in our head that it's not fun. *Tough.* Change the narrative, put on your manager hat, help the head of business development to start bringing in revenue, and positively remind them, "I'm not paying for you guys to sit there looking at Facebook all day." If you don't think you like it, find a way to put a positive spin on business development.

Be aware of pitfalls. The biggest potential opportunities and pitfalls during the first six months for you will be in the behaviors you establish or don't establish. We can all be masters of rationalization. We can convince ourselves of almost anything, even when it sabotages our success and works against our own best interest. Knowing that ahead of time, you must keep your investor hat on and remain laser-focused on accomplishing tasks. No matter how much you want to listen to an entertaining podcast or spend the day on your logo, nothing matters if you don't get the clients who bring in revenue. Work your plan and ensure you're hitting your business development metrics.

Schedule and time block your tasks and do them. There may be tasks you don't like doing or ones you feel you're horrible at. It's like doing sit-ups. Change the narrative in your head and know they will be worth it in the long run! Try not to feel overwhelmed with these new tasks and roles, as there is a light at the end of the tunnel. For now, you are the chief bottle washer, chef, server, and owner.

At this point, you might be saying, "Oh my god, I just don't want to do sales. We had a whole sales department. I'm not a salesman. This is going to suck!" The good news is that sales—when done well—will only be a major part of your journey for a short time. Once you've built a consistent client base and perform amazing work, sales will transition because clients will begin offering referrals. You will build a referral network instead of relying on cold calling. And eventually you can start to subcontract some of the roles you dislike. Embrace that you're changing the narrative in your head from "I have to" to "This is cool. I get to." There is a big difference between thinking "I have to do this" and "I *get* to do this." This thinking will be reflected in the work you do, how you do it, and how it is received.

These first six months, consistency is key. Remember your true motivation and your *why* for doing this. It's most important that you show up every day. Put on your suit, walk into your home office, shut your door, make calls, and kick ass.

FIND AN ACCOUNTABILITY PARTNER
You should expect that your new business is going to

feel like a different job because you're working *on* your business; it *is* a different job. Your work may be centered around business development, compliance, and running the business and less on being the technician. You can expect some ebb and flow, but in the beginning you likely won't be loaded with clients, which allows you to focus your free energy on building the business.

For some, these first six months can make you feel like you're alone on a deserted island. People who have a hard time with it can experience self-doubt and begin to think, "What did I just do?" Joining networking groups— or other like-minded communities—or signing up for one of my Solopreneur Success Camps allows you to share these negative thoughts and get encouragement and collaboration from others. You no longer have an office water cooler or common workplace to gather, and likely your old work colleagues won't understand the business aspects of what you're experiencing. To them, it's like you are suddenly talking a different language.

For accountability purposes, you could hire a business coach or find someone you trust. The person you are look-ing for may be one of the original business owners you spoke with. Or you could check in with your advisors to see if they have any suggestions.

You could ask your partner/spouse—however, I would

urge caution around using a loved one because it's all too easy for them to let you off the hook. If you do ask a loved one to be your accountability partner, set clear expectations for both roles.

An accountability partner will help hold you to the metrics you established on your goal board. Search for one who will hold your feet to the fire by requiring you to report on the tasks you fulfilled each week toward your goals. Set a time and day for the weekly call. Schedule these calls and take them seriously.

You and your accountability partner will check in and ensure you're meeting your commitments and accomplishing those tasks. "Where are you with task X? What are you getting done with job Y? How much have you gotten done on paperwork Z?" It needs to be someone you respect and don't want to let down, as the social pressure of having to be truthful and accountable will help you accomplish tasks. This may be another solopreneur or business owner.

Some people set up two-way accountability partnerships where each person provides accountability for the other— unlike a coach or mentor with whom the accountability is one-way. Accountability calls are not intended to turn into a "bitch session." They should be where you firmly and positively hold each other accountable and then help each other to problem solve.

In your initial meeting, tell your accountability partner specifically what you want them to help you with and check on. You have to guide them, and they have to know they can't let you off the hook. The more open and honest you can be here, the better. If you know you are concerned about completing a specific task, let them know that and why.

At aspiringsolopreneur.com I offer groups that hold monthly virtual meetings via video conference to help solopreneurs anywhere. In most cases these are professionally facilitated and offer an environment focused on confidentiality, learning, peer accountability, and group problem solving. Members have access to each other and to the facilitators offline. This way members know they can communicate with others in case they need to reach out. Participants have access to a private LinkedIn group, and I have ongoing coaching available as well.

The importance of finding a support system shouldn't be underestimated. Find your place to share and vent, "I made thirty calls today, and nobody called me back." Most people don't care, but somebody else who has done that in the past, or who is doing the same thing at the moment, *does care*, and they want to talk about their experience too. This also works when you want to share the successes that only someone with that same experience can appreciate. "Hey, I just landed a huge account that's going to pay me twice as much as I used to make!" Finding somebody that you can talk to is important, because those stories exist.

Having a good community will help you to problem solve, get better at what you do, and provide a place to commiserate the downs and celebrate the ups.

In our Solopreneur Success Camps, I walk people through all of the exercises in this book, engage in group coaching and problem solving, and hold them accountable. Through this group, they become a part of a solopreneur community group.

TAKEAWAYS

- Be aware of behavior pitfalls, and carefully time block to avoid them.
- Act like the investor, manager, and head of business development and focus on getting clients.
- Find an accountability partner and use accountability tools.

HOMEWORK

1. Set up time blocking to ensure you create good habits and drive sales.

2. Create your goal/dream board with dream photos and metrics.

3. Identify, write out, and schedule how you will hold yourself accountable via an accountability partner, time blocking, and weekly metrics.

CHAPTER SEVENTEEN

MAXIMIZE YOUR BANDWIDTH

———

Just because you can, doesn't mean you should.

SHERRILYN KENYON

In most cases, as time progresses, the technician role of your solopreneur life will become busier and you will need to start parsing your time more carefully. You will likely discover that marketing, bookkeeping, and government compliance issues are no longer the best use of your technician time.

Depending on your budget, you might be able to solicit help and outsource some of these tasks from the beginning. Or you might need to wait until you're seeing profits. Either way, at a minimum, for most solopreneur practices, the investor needs to manage the investment, the manager needs to manage, the head of business development needs to find new clients, and the technician role needs to actually execute on the work.

As you get increasingly busy, you'll have to acknowledge that you're not the best at everything or that you can contract it out for less than you can make as a technician. Ideally, you should spend the majority of time doing what you're great at, what makes you the happiest, and what generates revenue.

DELEGATION MATRIX

HOURLY VALUE OF TIME = TOTAL ANNUAL COMPENSATION ÷ 2000 HOURS / YEAR

HOURLY VALUE OF TIME $_____	WHAT YOU DO NOW "CURRENTLY DOING" $_____ COST / HOUR	SHOULD DO MORE "FOCUS" $_____ COST / HOUR	SHOULD DO LESS "CONTRACT OUT" $_____ COST / HOUR
LOVE IT GREAT AT IT			
LIKE IT GOOD AT IT			
OK OK			
HATE IT SUCK AT IT			
LOVE IT SUCK AT IT			

This Time Delegation and Allocation Matrix I created will help you to attach a dollar value to your time, assess where you should focus your energy, and identify what areas you can eventually delegate.

How do you begin this shift? Take a minute to calculate the rough hourly value of your time by taking your annual income divided by 2,000 hours—fifty-two weeks a year (minus two weeks of vacation) multiplied by an average forty hours a week. If you're making $100,000 net and divide that by 2,000, you've deemed your time is worth $50 an hour. Remember, you are likely billing much higher to cover costs, but this is a good way to estimate the value of your time. That means if you can get someone to do your bookkeeping for $30 an hour and you can generate $50 an hour or more as a technician, then you are better off to hire a bookkeeper and invest that time as a technician. You get to do what you're great at, what you love, and earn more money.

To decide what tasks to outsource, start by assessing what you do each week. Identify those tasks you love and hate, as well as what you're great at and what you stink at.

List them all in the spreadsheet and attach a rough dollar amount to each task. Then go through and input them into the delegation matrix. This should start to give you an idea of what to let go of. Invest more time at what you love, are great at, and gives a high dollar value. The goal is to spend more time there. Begin to identify any tasks to outsource. They may include bookkeeping, accounting, compliance, IT, scheduling, and paperwork. Look for other solopreneurs or a small firm that offers this type of support.

Make a plan to start to transition out of those tasks so you can focus more on what you love, are good at, and that earns revenue. You will still have to wear the manager hat, but you should contract out unnecessary use of your time, allowing you to wear the technician hat and earn an income.

SAVING MONEY BY HIRING A CONTRACTOR

Just because you *can* do something, doesn't mean that you *should*. I have the cleanest books in the world because I'm reasonably dyslexic with numbers. As a result of my challenges, I hired a professional bookkeeper from the very beginning. I could have done my own books, but it took an immense amount of time and I made many mistakes. It was a source of anxiety, so instead I found someone else who was good at the task and loved doing it. They were happy to handle the bookkeeping, and it empowered me to get out and be more productive elsewhere. In reality, learning this lesson was a great gift for me.

I once worked with a dentist who owned his own business. It wasn't a solo business as he needed a hygienist, an assistant, and people to run the office. The dentist was smart and could handle pretty much anything, including his marketing. This story applies to the solopreneur as a reminder that just because you can, doesn't mean you should.

I asked him, "How much are you paid as a dentist, working as a technician?" He earned approximately $300 per hour.

I asked how much time he spent doing marketing. "I only spend about five hours a week," he said.

I did the calculations and told him he could hire someone qualified and great to do marketing on a part-time basis for about $50 per hour or less. Therefore, doing his own marketing was costing him the difference at $250 per hour, or over $1000 a week. His time as a dentist was worth more, and he needed to outsource the task, which would free up some of his time and drive more cash to the bottom line—his ultimate goal.

When you do decide to contract things out, keep in mind you are now acting like a manager again. Remember, don't allow people to work without any direction. People aren't psychic. Give clear expectations of your contractors, be clear on communication, and have clear processes for accountability.

Looking at the matrix, outsource the items that you hate, aren't good at, and can afford. Then move higher. Ideally, you want to focus your time on the tasks that generate the most income and make you the happiest. Don't discard the things you love to do but aren't very good at—just transition those into hobbies!

MAXIMUM BANDWIDTH

Humans have a maximum amount of bandwidth. Imagine an engine that runs in the red zone at 130 percent for a time period. The engine can sustain that pace for a while, but then eventually explodes. As a human, you can run in that red zone, sometimes for a long time, but if you continue too long, bad things are going to happen. You will burn out. You will make mistakes. You will snap. Remember this wasn't the reason you became a solopreneur.

You might say it's okay to keep up a manic pace since you're making a significant amount of money and it's your own business now. However, if you're earning this money by working ninety hours a week again, you're essentially back on the hamster wheel. Put on your manager hat and find a way to free up time. You're obligated, wearing your investor hat, to protect your investment. You, as the technician, are the investment—so delegate where necessary and focus on maximizing the greatest return for the long haul.

TIME WELL SPENT

Make sure that all time is being well spent. Be properly engaged during work time *and* off time. It's necessary to separate your solopreneur life and home life. I believe that balance is important so that when you leave your home office, you shut the door and you are no longer working. It's important to your family and your clients that you recharge your batteries in a way that you can be your best to everyone in your life.

If you're completely burnt out in your off time, then you can't function properly and productively at work. Start to consider how you spend all of your time. If you've defined your time is worth $50 an hour, is it worth that amount to watch your kid's soccer game? Absolutely. Is it worth $50 an hour watching late night infomercials for three hours by yourself? Probably not.

Wear your investor and manager hats and do everything possible to protect the person wearing the head of business development and technician hats because the technician is the asset of the business. Lead a balanced, well-rounded life that makes you feel happy and energetic.

That's why you are on this journey.

THE DELEGATION MATRIX OF YOUR LIFE

You want to make sure that during the hours you're not working that your time is spent toward making a better, happier, more energized *you*. Another analogy I like is about being an airplane passenger. The flight attendant says, "In the unlikely event of loss of cabin pressure, put your oxygen mask on first, *before you try to help others*." In life, as in an airplane, put your "oxygen mask" on first in order to be a great dad, a great mom, a great business owner, or a great technician. You must take care of yourself.

Many people often want to put others first. That may not be the best option, and when you consider you're not wearing only four hats, but you're probably wearing *many* hats in life—a parent to children, an adult child of aging parents, a neighbor, a partner/spouse—and you need to be the best *you* possible in order to be happy and successful. Address your stress, watch how and where you're spending your time, and be the best *you* that *you* can be. All the people you interact with, under all the different hats, deserve it.

You may consider applying the delegation matrix to your nonbusiness activities, as you may be surprised how you can realign your "off time."

PRO TIP: DON'T BORROW TO SAVE

When you start out, you're going to have to define with your investor and manager roles if contracting tasks out is the best thing for you or if you can stay busy producing income as a technician.

Eventually you may hire somebody to do your book-keeping, marketing, and IT. Maybe in your personal life you'll hire people to mow the lawn, clean the house, and pick up your laundry. However, when you are starting out, I don't suggest that you borrow money to contract out the things you don't want to do. Instead, constantly reevaluate and use the matrix as your situation improves.

You built a timeline, launched your solopreneur life, and had metrics to know what success would look like. You can follow the same steps to calculate what you'll contract out when you hit X dollars and bottom-line profit. Use your dream board and the items represented as a reward for being able to start delegating. Celebrate that success and begin to outsource the things you don't want to be doing. As an example, you may tell yourself, "When I get to thirty hours a week of consistent technician production, I will then contract out my marketing efforts."

You will see an ebb and flow on the demands of your time. At times you'll be working more, and then you'll need to work smart. Focus on how you're going to achieve the goals you want.

EXTRICATE YOURSELF

It's not always easy to step away from something, but often you can do it little by little. Make a plan and a time-line for transitioning the task to someone else. If you don't make a plan, you'll likely never do it. People who become solopreneurs are often educated and experts in their field. They've been told their entire lives that they can handle anything. This may be true, but now it's time to take a step back and ask yourself how much each little thing is costing you, both in time and/or treasure (dollars) and if it's the best use of your talent. Where are you getting in your own way?

Sometimes people continue to perform tasks themselves because they think that a hired contractor won't do the job as well as they do it. In that case, stop being a control freak, and accept that others simply may do things *differently*. If you hired an accountant who doesn't know how to submit the proper IRS forms, you're likely in trouble. They are not the right person. If, however, the forms are precisely completed but the accountant uses blue ink instead of black, you can do your job and let them do theirs. Choose your team and your battles wisely.

TAKEAWAYS

- With your investor or manager hat on, it's your job to protect and maximize the dollars coming in. You will need to manage your head of business development and technician time.
- You can calculate the value of your time and use this

value to assess and allocate where you should focus that time and determine what you can let go of.

- To maximize bandwidth, build a plan to contract out work that isn't the highest and best use of your time.

HOMEWORK

1. Use the delegation matrix to assess your strengths and what is the highest and best use of your time.
2. Based on finances and time, make a plan to contract out the work that you dislike and aren't as good at.
3. Schedule a quarterly refresh of the delegation matrix to ensure you are achieving the highest return on your efforts.

CONCLUSION

FINDING YOUR TRUE BALANCE

———

I want you to go into your venture eyes wide open, to be crystal clear on your thinking as an investor, manager, head of business development, and technician with a clear plan for a smooth, successful transition. Ready to dive in and thrive. You're ready now.

Your awareness will allow you to be a shrewd investor and decide with your investor hat on whether this business represents the highest and best use of your time, treasure, and talent.

REMIND YOURSELF

It's important to review your motivations and remind yourself why you wanted to be a solopreneur in the first place. Likely you have been a great technician your entire life, and you were taught the only way to make more money was to work more and do everything yourself. Now you know that's no longer true! You can embrace a new way of thinking, make more money, and work less.

It's no cliché when I say that I want to see you realize your dreams and fulfill your motivations and dreams. It's 100 percent possible. I like the old expression, "Nobody ever lay on their deathbed wishing they had worked more." If you can hold yourself accountable, you can have it all. More time. More money. Higher profile.

I have a friend who attends all of his kids' games. Being there for his kids at their games is really important to him, and he's been able to create a life that allows him to do that. He may not have the biggest house in the world, but he works much smarter than if he let himself be forced into someone else's schedule. He has financial freedom, low stress, gets to do what he loves, see his kids, and lives his best life.

If you want to take the day off, that's your call. You won't have to ask for permission. You're likely not being paid, but you're fulfilling your primary goal of spending time with your family. You as a technician can take the day off, but make sure you're wearing your investor hat too. You are now fully accountable for all the roles.

Accountability allows you to find your own balance in your work and in your life. If you're working too much and starting to get wound up, stress and anxiety will make it more difficult to be a great technician. You may need extra resources. This is where you reach out to your board of advisors or to an accountability group, or a person to talk to outside of your family and outside of your business. Having someone, or a group, to share your particular issues with can help you handle the stress and move forward. You will need someone to bounce things off of because when you're in the thick of it—good or bad—you don't want to be stuck in your own echo chamber. I recommend that as you launch your solopreneur career you have some system in place to step out of your head and share with others who know what you're going through. Make sure you find that support group, accountability partner, or join us at aspiringsolopreneur.com.

MY FORCED REASSESSMENT

A few years ago, I had a hip and knee replacement that resulted in a lot of forced downtime. I'm not good at downtime, but it gave me a great opportunity for reflection and contemplation. I reconsidered my definition of success and happiness. My wife and I had a great marriage, money was okay, and we liked where we lived. We decided to define what our next chapter would be and make plans for our future.

My wife and I made a conscious decision to live in a simple house on a great lot that backs up to woods and a lake. I try to hike or walk almost every day, which is a great way to clear my head, help me focus, and approach everything in a more positive way. Many of our friends and peers have much bigger, grander houses, and that's okay with us. I've never had a car payment, and I've never owned a new car because it seems like a waste of money to me. We are not judging; it's just that this approach works for us and we keep it simple. My wife and I decided that we don't ever want to retire. We love what we do that much, and it's part of who we are. In our experience, people who retire often seem to suddenly age and to lose their purpose in life.

We have planned to not retire because we love our work and we want to continue having adventures. Travel and fitness are priorities for us, the places where we like to invest our time and treasure. We travel almost every month and typically take a month-long adventure in the summer. I just completed my second 50K ultramarathon and have more scheduled out. Because we took the time to intentionally make those plans, we adjusted our life to fit them, and we are now embracing our best life. As a result, this focus and clarity has empowered us to work fewer hours with more revenue and more adventure than ever before.

This book is a direct result of the time I took for reflection. You may go through this process many times. I have! Reset your goals and keep striving for life on your terms. I know that you can achieve anything you can dream of... and I hope you dream big.

CELEBRATE THE VICTORY

I hope this book leads you to expand your ideas about what you can accomplish. Think about your priorities and the things that you would like to do and feel a need to do. Not goals or priorities from your parents, peers, or society, but from your own heart.

If your priority is to be the greatest dad or mom in the world, that's wonderful. It's well within your power. If it's to write a book that makes an impact on people, great. If it's to be a rock star in some field, or a phenomenal golfer, or financially wealthy beyond your imagination, strive for that goal. Maybe it means simplifying your life and taking control to become a solopreneur. This thinking may enable you to change your mode of thinking about success and achievement. What are your dreams? Do them!

You have undertaken the massive shift required to begin your successful solopreneur journey and you deserve huge kudos. This is important because, speaking as a former Midwest martyr—someone who works eighty hours a week and tells everyone how busy and buried they are—we often suck at celebrating victories. I hope you take a minute and realize that it's a victory to have read this book and embraced the ideas in it.

Celebrate the victory that you stopped and explored something that was uncomfortable and maybe even a little scary. Maybe a solopreneur life feels right for you, and maybe it doesn't. Take a couple of victory laps for stopping to consider it for yourself. On that alone, you are part of a unique breed of people who would not just talk about doing something but do the deep dive into the activities required to consider what it would look like in *real life*.

Maybe you went through the activities and you realized that your first idea won't work, but *you still want to work for yourself*. I want you to be excited because the activities made you start thinking in a way that you never thought before. You turned on thinking that you may not have had before. Next, you'll start seeing new opportunities everywhere, and that's when you pick this book up and start over again. Come back to the book and wash, rinse, and repeat until you find your no-brainer.

WHAT'S NEXT

I hope that this book has taught you to question everything, educate yourself, and to learn to become an expert. Start adapting and adopting this approach in other areas of your life. Look for our new book, *What's Next in Life.*

These ideas can be tools that you learn here and then use to help your family. Maybe you want to take a year off and live overseas. Any new venture can be considered using the same rubric. Repeat the themes of these activities, and you'll find they are tools that you can use and hone. If you have children, teach them these ideas and concepts since they are a rational way to approach any project. I believe this could be the greatest gift you could possibly give to the next generation.

If your children are college-aged, encourage them to use the system to think critically about postsecondary education. Instead of planning to go to college because everyone else goes, they can approach their future purposefully. Do they want to go to college? Have them research available choices. Encourage your kids to use this thinking as their foundation and springboard for any life choice.

This book has offered you a new skillset and way of thinking. With these ideas you can better identify your ambitions and move them further ahead. I believe that our own thinking can be the greatest inhibitor or enabler of our success and that greatness often lives in the fringe of the reasonable.

We live in an abundant age, and *if you can think it, you can make it happen.* If you believe it, it's just a matter of identifying that *belief* and then breaking it down into its pieces. Figure out the components necessary to get there and to make it work. The only limit to your dreams is *you.*

I invite you to explore aspiringsolopreneur.com and learn what it's about. We embrace people living their best solopreneur life and provide the tools and resources to help solopreneurs thrive.

Entrepreneurship and self-employment have come along ways since the 1980s.

During my journey, I've made many mistakes and I've had many victories. It has been an amazing journey. I believe it's worth all the effort to get there and most people are skilled in their trade—they just need some help with the process of building a solopreneur life. I know you can.

Connect with us and share your stories—your success and failures—at aspiringsolopreneur.com.

Thank you from the bottom of my heart for giving your treasured time to read this. Keep smiling.

Welcome to the revolution.

—Kris

APPENDIX

LIFE BALANCE WHEEL REVIEW

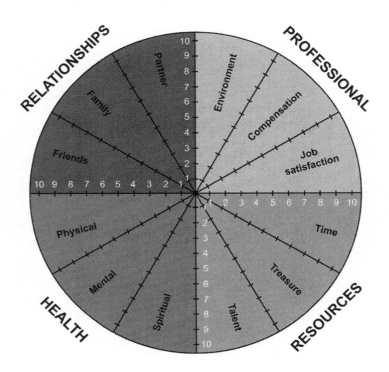

This questionnaire is intended to help expand your thinking on how you define "success." Success on your terms. Going forward, you will be the boss, and it will be important for you to know where you're going. As you work through this, know that there isn't any right or wrong answer. Be open and dive in. If your score seems a bit low, get excited to know you're identifying areas in which you can improve. If you have sections that score high, celebrate them as victories.

This knowledge will help you to define what your ideal solopreneur life may look like. Once you know this, you can begin to back into what you will need to do to achieve it.

All questions are rated on a scale of 1–10, with 10 indicating you're getting the maximum level of satisfaction from that particular aspect and/or that you agree with the statement.

RELATIONSHIPS

Partner:	Score
I'm satisfied with this relationship.	
We've set clear goals and plans for our future together.	
We're open and honest in our communications.	
I'm supportive of my partner's needs and goals.	
My partner is supportive of my needs and goals.	

Family:	
I'm satisfied with these relationships.	
We're open and honest in our communications.	
I know the goals of my family members, and I support and help them in achieving them.	
I ask questions and actively listen when in conversation.	
I feel I'm heard when communicating with my family.	

Friends:	
I'm satisfied with my current level of friendships.	
I'm open and honest in my communications with my friends.	
I personally meet with friends at a frequency I like.	
My partner and I meet with friends at a frequency we like.	
I'm happy with the degree and engagement level of my friendships.	

Relationships Total	
Divide by 15	
Multiply by 10	
RELATIONSHIPS PERCENTAGE	

PROFESSIONAL

Environment:	Score
I feel happy and comfortable in my workplace.	
I like and respect the people with whom I work, and I believe they like and respect me.	
I feel like my workplace supports both my personal and professional growth.	
I understand the direction of the organization and how I'm contributing to achieving the overall goal.	
My workplace's values align with my personal values.	

Compensation:	
I believe that I'm paid what I deserve for my efforts.	
I have the amount of time off and flexibility I desire.	
My skills are being utilized to their highest and best use.	
I have a clearly defined path for growth and advancement.	
I receive the level of training I want; if not, I have the support of the organization to obtain more training.	

Job Satisfaction:	
I enjoy the work I do, and I like going to work.	
I enjoy my coworkers.	
There are specific and clear expectations of me and my responsibilities.	
I have clear metrics that enable me to determine if I'm successful.	
I understand how my contributions impact the overall success of the organization.	

Professional Total	
Divide by 15	
Multiply by 10	
PROFESSIONAL PERCENTAGE	

RESOURCES

Time:	Score
I feel I have enough time to complete all my work and daily tasks.	
I take as much vacation time as I want.	
I have enough time to attend events that support others.	
I invest time daily for my own clarity and physical exercise.	
I take time to invest in my own personal growth.	

Treasure:	
I have all the right "stuff" I need to live my best life.	
I could comfortably go without an income for at least six months.	
My financial stability enables me to live the life I desire.	
My "stuff" (house, car, etc.) supports the best life I want to live.	
My financial and work lives aren't focused on supporting my "stuff."	

Talent:	
I feel I've found my true natural talents in life.	
I currently embrace and utilize these talents to their full potential.	
I take the time I need to develop and improve these talents.	
Others are aware of the talents I possess.	
I have a clear plan to maximize and benefit from these talents.	

Resources Total	
Divide by 15	
Multiply by 10	
RESOURCES PERCENTAGE	

HEALTH

Physical:	Score

I'm happy with my level of physical activity and fitness.

While alone, standing naked in front of a
mirror, I'm pleased with my appearance.

I invest the time daily to make my physical health a priority.

I have a healthy relationship with what I eat and drink.

I'm confident the vices I choose to embrace have
minimal negative impact on my health.

Mental:

I'm happy with my current level of mental health.

I'm pleased with who I am and confident with where I'm going.

I like the people I surround myself with.

I rarely have feelings of dread or worry.

I invest time daily to provide myself
with clarity and peace of mind.

Spiritual:

I'm happy with my definition and understanding of "spirituality."

My spiritual beliefs are in alignment with how I live my life.

I've surrounded myself with others who share my spiritual beliefs.

I make important life decisions based on these beliefs.

My spiritual beliefs help me find purpose and direction in my life.

Health Total

Divide by 15

Multiply by 10

HEALTH PERCENTAGE

At this point, go back to the Balance Wheel illustration. Imagine that you'd have a perfectly round wheel (a ranking of 10 for each question) if each of the sections resulted in the same score. If your score in one section is high, yet low in another, you'll have an uneven Balance Wheel. This suggests you have opportunities to improve. Wonderful; you will be the boss, so how can you achieve this?

Looking at each area, ask yourself what *amazing* would look like for each answer and write them out. From here you will start to dream bigger and define success. You can go to our site aspiringsolopreneur.com for a video that walks you through how to do this exercise.

By reviewing the results of this activity, you'll be able to recognize where you should focus your attention to improve a currently low score. As a reminder, this tool is simply intended to aid you in identifying what success looks like—on your terms. As a successful solopreneur, you don't live in a box—you can have it all. But first you have to define what you really want and begin to outline what it will take to achieve it. Write it down and be as specific as you can. I believe something amazing happens when we take the time to clearly see what success looks like in our mind's eye and document it.

If you'd like further clarification on this activity, please feel free to go to aspiringsolopreneur.com and watch the video.

READING LIST

———

I have been a student of entrepreneurship, personal accountability, and learning my entire life. This goes back to my early childhood and started with reading the different merit badge books that were required for me to achieve my first LCG, the rank of Eagle Scout. This, and from my dad, is where I first learned about goal-setting. Since that time, I have read—or more likely listened to—thousands of books, articles, lectures, and podcasts. I participated in one of the earlier College Entrepreneurial programs in the country in the 1980s and proceeded to consume as much information on entrepreneurship, leadership, and business as possible...information that helped to shape my thinking, experiences, and the thoughts in this book.

In most cases, the ideas in these books have likely been shaped by others. It is with my wholehearted appreciation for this thinking and the ideas conveyed that I would hope that others build on what I have produced.

Here is a list (albeit not anywhere near comprehensive) of influencers who have authored some additional reading that I have found to be of value.

In order of date of publication:

- Sun Tzu, *The Art of War,* fifth century BC
- Adam Smith, *The Wealth of Nations,* March 9, 1776
- Ernest Shackleton, *South: A Memoir of the* Endurance *Voyage,* 1919
- Dale Carnegie, *How to Win Friends and Influence People,* October 1936
- F. A. Hayek, *The Road to Serfdom,* March 1944
- Norman Vincent Peale, *The Power of Positive Thinking,* 1952
- Norman Vincent Peale, *Enthusiasm Makes the Difference,* 1967
- Norman Vincent Peale, *You Can If You Think You Can,* 1974
- Michael E. Porter, *Competitive Strategy: Techniques for Analyzing Industries and Competitors,* 1980
- Allen Carr, *Easy Way to Stop Smoking,* 1985
- Michael E. Gerber, *The E Myth: Why Most Businesses Don't Work and What to Do About It,* 1986
- Paul Hawken, *Growing a Business,* 1987
- Stephen R. Covey, *The 7 Habits of Highly Effective People,* August 15, 1989
- Dan Sullivan, *How The Best Get Better,* 1996

- Paulo Coelho, *Warrior of the Light: A Manual*, 1997
- Robert T. Kiyosaki, *Rich Dad Poor Dad: What the Rich Teach Their Kids about Money That the Poor and Middle Class Do Not!*, 1997
- Jim Collins, *Good to Great: Why Some Companies Make the Leap...and Others Don't*, 2001
- Patrick Lencioni, *The Five Dysfunctions of a Team: A Leadership Fable*, 2002
- Patrick Lencioni, *Death by Meeting: A Leadership Fable...about Solving the Most Painful Problem in Business*, 2004
- Steve Farber, *The Radical Leap: A Personal Lesson in Extreme Leadership*, 2004
- Dan Sullivan and Catherine Nomura, *The Laws of Lifetime Growth: Always Make Your Future Bigger Than Your Past*, 2006
- Steve Farber, *The Radical Edge: Stoke Your Business, Amp Your Life, and Change the World*, 2006
- Timothy Ferriss, *The 4-hour Workweek: Escape 9–5, Live Anywhere, and Join the New Rich*, April 24, 2007
- Matt Ridley, *The Rational Optimist: How Prosperity Evolves*, May 18, 2010
- Tommy Spaulding, *It's Not Just Who You Know: Transform Your Life (and Your Organization) by Turning Colleagues and Contacts into Lasting, Genuine Relationships*, August 10, 2010
- Greg McKeown, *Essentialism: The Disciplined Pursuit of Less*, December 31, 2014

- Patrick Lencioni, *The Advantage: Why Organizational Health Trumps Everything Else in Business*, 2012
- Dan Sullivan, *The 80% Approach*, 2013
- Gary Keller and Jay Papasan, *The ONE Thing: The Surprisingly Simple Truth Behind Extraordinary Results*, April 1, 2013
- Gino Wickman, *Traction: Get a Grip on Your Business*, 2011
- Tommy Spaulding, *The Heart-Led Leader: How Living and Leading from the Heart Will Change Your Organization and Your Life*, October 6, 2015
- Jocko Willink and Leif Babin, *Extreme Ownership: How U.S. Navy SEALs Lead and Win*, October 20, 2015
- Brian Tracy, *Get Smart!: How to Think and Act Like the Most Successful and Highest-Paid People in Every Field*, March 5, 2016
- Patrick Lencioni, *The Ideal Team Player: How to Recognize and Cultivate the Three Essential Virtues, A Leadership Fable*, April 25, 2016
- Simon Sinek with David Mead and Peter Docker, *Find Your WHY: A Practical Guide for Discovering Purpose for You and Your Team*, September 5, 2017
- Brian Tracy and Christina Stein, *Believe It to Achieve It: Overcome Your Doubts, Let Go of the Past, and Unlock Your Full Potential*, 2017

And so many, many more. Thank you all.

ACKNOWLEDGMENTS

———

To all the brave solopreneurs, entrepreneurs, business owners, leaders, managers, and technicians who are embracing life on their terms: what I have learned and continue to learn from you can't be measured.

To all the people who supported and empowered the creation of this book, the aspiringsolopreneur.com site, and the solopreneur success programs: it is because of your efforts that we will introduce at least a million people to a new way of thinking and change lives. I am grateful and humbled by the passion and support of each and every person involved.

Thank you to all the people who contributed content to this book: the experts willing to share their time and thoughts for our interviews, and all the experts in their respective fields from whom I have learned so much.

Without your combined contributions, this book would not have the impact I hope it will.

From the bottom of my heart.

Thank you.

ABOUT THE AUTHOR

___

KRIS KLUVER is a seasoned entrepreneur with over 30 years of experience, who started his first of 14 companies at age nineteen. Since then, he has been involved with businesses ranging from business consulting to real estate, online services, counseling, advertising, financial services, and many more. A former business broker and current strategic advisor and mentor, Kris has seen the inner workings of hundreds of businesses, some good, some ugly, all interesting. Through his many experiences, he has gained a unique understanding, appreciation, and love of solopreneurship along with a genuine passion for helping others achieve their dreams.

51780741R00207

Made in the USA
Lexington, KY
05 September 2019